The Evaluation Interview

Fifth Edition

How to Probe Deeply,
Get Candid Answers, and
Predict the Performance of Job
Candidates

Richard A. Fear
Robert J. Chiron

McGraw-Hill

New York Chicago San Francisco Lisbon London
Madrid Mexico City Milan New Delhi San Juan
Seoul Singapore Sydney Toronto

McGraw-Hill

A Division of The McGraw·Hill Companies

Copyright © 2002, 1990 by The McGraw-Hill Companies, Inc. All rights reserved. Printed in the United States of America. Except as permitted under the United States Copyright Act of 1976, no part of this publication may be reproduced or distributed in any form or by any means, or stored in a database or retrieval system, without the prior written permission of the publisher.

1 2 3 4 5 6 7 8 9 0 DOC/DOC 0 9 8 7 6 5 4 3 2

ISBN 0-07-137791-3

Library of Congress Cataloging-in-Publication Data applied for.

The sponsoring editor is Richard Narramore. Production services provided by CWL Publishing Enterprises, Madison, Wisconsin, www.cwlpub.com.

Printed and bound by R. R. Donnelley & Sons Company.

McGraw-Hill books are available at special quantity discounts to use as premiums and sales promotions, or for use in corporate training programs. For more information, please write to the Director of Special Sales, McGraw-Hill, 2 Penn Plaza, New York, NY 10121. Or contact your local bookstore.

 This book is printed on recycled, acid-free paper containing a minimum of 50% recycled de-inked fiber.

|Contents

iii

Preface to the Fifth Edition

S till in print after 40 years, *The Evaluation Interview* now occupies an important place in most of the human resources offices in North America, and in many English-speaking countries throughout the world. I believe one of the reasons the book has been so successful is that the interviewing techniques it describes have many applications outside the hiring interview. Managers who have been trained in interviewing using *The Evaluation Interview* as a guide find themselves utilizing the techniques not only for selection of new staff but for many other day-to-day activities. They discover that they draw upon their interviewing skills in their discussions with sub-contractors, union officials, subordinates, and even with superiors.

Wherever they are faced with situations in everyday life that place a premium on drawing the other person out, finding out what is on that person's mind and analyzing the responses, students of this book have a genuine advantage.

Over time, we have seen how versatile *The Evaluation Interview* training techniques really are. Take the example of a major *Fortune* 50 company that was having difficulty with its customer interviews. For years these had been completed in over two hours, with little information gained and customers annoyed with the lengthy process. With this feedback in hand, we adapted the principles of *The Evaluation Interview* and re-engineered the process to 30 minutes. Feedback from the participants in this process was outstanding. They were gaining more insights in a shorter time than they had ever done before. All we did was to adapt the process to meet their needs.

In this, the Fifth Edition of *The Evaluation Interview*, we capitalize on what we have learned over the past 11 years since the Fourth Edition was published, while keeping the basic principles intact; they are as useful today as they were when they were developed over 40 years ago.

$$* \quad * \quad *$$

As the original author, I have made a great many selection decisions over a long life, but none so important as my selection of Dr. Robert Chiron to carry on for me after retirement and to co-author this book. Dr. Chiron has brought innovation to a long-established process. He has set the book on fire with many exciting applications, ranging from creating "alignment" and "fit" in organizations to succession planning and team building. He brings even more to the table in this Fifth Edition.

—Richard Fear, March 2002

The Fifth Edition of *The Evaluation Interview* is dedicated to the over half century of work that Richard Fear has contributed to the process of evaluation interviewing. No single person has had the impact Dick has had in this area. It is a privilege for me to carry the mantle of integrity and thoroughness of this approach.

Many thanks to Fred Rosen for his contributions in editing this manuscript. And, as always, a big thank-you to my family, who make everything I do worthwhile.

—Robert Chiron, March 2002
Rjc3340@aol.com

Part One | Before the Interview

Chapter One | An Overview of the Evaluation Interview

Organizations need to hire people with potential for growth. That is what this book is all about. A company can gain competitive advantage by supplying superior products and service, but at the heart of it all are people. People, not organizations, create and innovate. People make the difference in products and service. People, in the final analysis, determine whether a business succeeds or fails. To be competitive, a business must learn to utilize the untapped creative potential of the most powerful competitive weapons it has—its employees.

THE TEN MOST COMMON MISTAKES INTERVIEWERS MAKE

Since interviewing is an art, subject to the individual's interpretative questions, it is easy to fall into bad habits and come to an interview unprepared. We are all human, and it is easy to get sloppy and take shortcuts just to finish the process.

Over the years, we have observed a wide spectrum of interviewing practices. We have captured what we believe are the 10 most common mistakes interviewers make. They are not necessarily in order of priority, but they are all-important to be aware of in conducting a proper assessment.

1. Failure to Prepare and Organize for the Interview

Preliminary work needs to be done on the job description and the skills necessary to accomplish the job. Too often interviewers come to the interview without having done this work, and as a result they do not get an accurate assessment of the candidate, and the interview ends up being too general. Skills, traits, and knowledge needed for the position should be well documented, so that specific questions can be asked that will gain insight into those areas.

There are also physical preparations that increase the value of the interview. Setting up the room so that the interviewee is at the head of the table with the interviewer at the side allows for "line of sight" communications, as compared to sitting across from the candidate, which creates a physical barrier to communications.

2. Failure to Establish Rapport and Trust, and Failure to Put the Person at Ease

It is important to set the ground rules at the outset with respect to purpose, process, and timing. Let the individual know what to expect from the interview and how it will be conducted. Knowing this structure can help put a person at ease so that he or she will speak more candidly and not just give formulaic responses designed to create a positive impression. To help an interviewee open up, the interviewer should begin with an "ice breaker" that will help the person feel at ease.

Rapport is central to the evaluation interview, so that the individual does not feel you are judging him or her. Your goal should be to respond to the interviewee with "unconditional positiveness" and encourage the interviewee to tell you everything about himself or herself without prejudging whether it is good or bad. By utilizing this psychological principle we are able to get a better and truer picture of the person.

Rapport is useful throughout the interview process. It is important, however, to start this early and maintain it in order to help the individual feel comfortable about you and about the process. Remember, for most people an interview is an unstructured process with which they have had little training or practice, so the more structure, trust, and rapport is built in, the more information you will get.

Watch your tone. Too often interviewers are so stiff and formal early in the interview that they do not establish rapport. The interviewer must spend time encouraging the interviewee in order to put the person at ease. *Whenever an individual says something that he or she is proud of, or indicates an accomplishment, say "Good for you," or "It appears you are proud of that accomplishment."* You will elicit more information, and the individual will feel more comfortable telling you his or her story.

Using both non-verbal reinforcement (a nodding of the head, looking interested) and verbal reinforcement is invaluable throughout the process. Additionally, by encouraging early, you will set the stage and reinforce yourself in continuing to do so throughout the interview. This becomes a positive conditioning response for the interviewer as well as for the interviewee, and information will flow more freely.

3. Failure to Use Simple Language and Open-Ended Questions

One of the biggest mistakes interviewers make is asking closed-ended questions instead of open-ended questions. Any questions that begin with "Did you," "Have you," or "Are you" are examples of closed-ended questions. Any question whose response is a "yes" or "no" is a closed-ended question because it does not give you any information about the individual. While a question like "Do you believe in treating people fairly?" seems open-ended because it asks for interpretation, it really is not. What person would answer "No"? This is really a leading question, because you are giving the individual the answer that is perceived to be correct or right.

Any question that asks for real thinking and interpretation is open-ended. "What are your specific job strengths?" "How would you solve a problem that involves two strong-willed subordinates?" "What has been your biggest problem in attaining your career goals?" These are all examples of open-ended questions because they require the individual to think and interpret. Interviewers may like to ask closed-ended questions because they produce quick responses, but these kinds of questions do not add materially to what is learned about the person.

It is also important to use simple language in asking questions. This is not the time to use an extensive vocabulary so that a person does not understand what you are asking. Questions need to be brief and to the point. This is called "economy of expression."

4. Failure to Listen and the Need to Talk

Most people love to talk, but few people really enjoy *listening*. Coach Lou Holtz once said, "Success comes from listening. I have never learned anything from talking."

Sometimes interviewers want to tell the individual all about themselves as a way to develop rapport and put a person at ease, then spend the last few minutes learning about the individual. This is a mistake. The intent is to get the individual talking, which means that the interviewer's role is that of a facilitator and/or coach.

In this process, the interviewee does about 85% of the talking. The focus is on the candidate. The role of the interviewer is to ask probing, open-ended questions in order to get at the relevant information required to do the assessment. Listen to what is said and what is not said. Do not ask loaded questions like "So you think that being direct with people is bad?" Giving the individual the answers does not help you to assess what the person is really like and what his or her needs really are.

5. Failure to Follow up on Questions to Understand the "Whys" behind the "Whats"

Most interviewers do a good job of getting at the "what" a person does, but they rarely get at the "why" behind the "what." What they learn about is where a person has worked and the nature of the job, but they do not get at the specific roles and responsibilities of the individual and the impact and influence those roles had on the job. Most people speaking about their former jobs tend to generalize, and so we end up learning more about their former companies than we do about their accomplishments and skills.

There is a tendency, early on in the training and development of interviewers, to move methodically from one question to the other in order to finish the interview. Interviewers tend to be more concerned with completing the task than they are with what they are learning about the individual. It is critical to understand the motivations and reasons behind what a person does in order to evaluate that person. The "why" allows you to measure motivation and maturity.

6. Failure to Control the Interview

It is easy to lose control of the interview. If you let people ramble on early and you encourage them to do so, they will be conditioned to continue talking. If information is not relevant to the job, then you must refocus the person using appropriate "control" techniques. If this is not done, an interview can last far too long.

Interviewers have a tendency to rush the interview or let it drag on. Especially when people are first trained to do interviews, their focus is on "task completion" versus "task completeness." There is a tendency to move from one question to the other without proper evaluation. Most people, when they are first trained, are satisfied just to finish the interview. They finish all right, but without fully understanding who the person is or what motivates them. This is the difference between a "descriptive" interview and an "evaluative" interview.

The "art" of this interview is to balance control with patience in order to get the relevant information needed to complete the assessment. This skill takes time to develop and comes with maturity in the interviewing process.

7. Failure to Get the Evidence

Some interviewers try to be psychoanalysts. We want to evaluate what we believe people are, but we let our preconceived beliefs cloud our objective judgment. It is an approach doomed to failure, because while it may be fun to analyze someone, that is not our job. Our job is to gather critical evidence of performance ability. Interviewers must watch the tendency to use their own past experiences in a vain attempt to evaluate people without the necessary, objective data to form conclusions.

8. Failure to Challenge One's Own Assumptions and Tendency to Jump to Conclusions

It is easy for interviewers, when they first meet their candidates, to draw first impressions and jump to conclusions. For example, if a candidate has a limp handshake and doesn't look directly at you, an interviewer might jump to the conclusion that the person is unassertive, is weak, or lacks personal forcefulness. In many instances the wrong conclusion would have been reached.

What if the person had broken his or her hand and the cast had just been taken off, or a person came from a different culture where eye contact was inappropriate? In these cases a wrong assessment would be made. But on the other hand, if an interviewer is favorably disposed to a candidate very early, this could result in evaluating the candidate too positively or, to compensate for that, pressing for shortcomings despite an initial favorable impression. It is important to remind yourself that your *first* impression is not your *last* impression. Never draw conclusions from one piece of data. That demonstrates disrespect for the individual and, in many cases, leads to making a wrong decision. The key is to challenge our own assumptions. Being aware of our personal biases helps to make a more objective assessment of the candidate. We have to continuously make sure that our own likes or dislikes do not color our perceptions.

9. Being Judgmental

Sometimes, as interviewers, we have a need to judge what people have said they have done and share it with them at that moment. If someone has taken six years to finish a degree, an interviewer might say, "Why did it take you so long to finish your degree? Did you not work hard enough, or were you distracted?" Saying this would be seen as negative. The candidate might then be cautious about answering future questions or sharing information openly with you at a later time. Rapport will have been jeopardized. You don't want people feeling they are being evaluated on every question.

10. Asking Questions Not Related to the Job

It is easy for interviewers to get sidetracked in areas that do not directly pertain to the job description and specifications. For example, if an individual talked about investments and financial planning as a job function and the interviewer was interested in specific investments, he or she might pose a question regarding those investments and the nature of the risk. Or, if an individual talked about something that was unrelated to the job, such as sports, an interviewer might ask questions in that area.

This is why it is critically important to have a job description that outlines the specific aspects of the job in question. The better the job is documented as to the skills, traits, and knowledge required, the more efficiently the interview can be focused.

Understanding and becoming familiar with these mistakes will enhance your ability to do an interview both effectively and efficiently, while maintaining rapport with the individual. Too often interviewers are asked to do an interview without the needed training to support their efforts. These 10 failures have been observed over and over again, so being aware of them early can only enhance the overall process.

Chapter Two | A Good Hiring Process Starts with a Good Job Description

It's no surprise that many organizations do not have adequate job descriptions. Nor do many have clear documentation about the kinds of behavior specifications they are seeking: those aptitudes, abilities, and personality traits essential for successful job performance. In fact, some companies have no job descriptions at all, and others like to keep them vague on purpose, to give themselves greater flexibility.

And yet accurate job descriptions and behavior specifications are absolutely fundamental to the development of any selection program. These two pieces of information should provide the basis for the development of the application form, the preliminary interview, the employment tests, and the employment interview itself. How can an interviewer evaluate the qualifications of an applicant without knowing what to look for?

JOB DESCRIPTION

A company's human resources department, in close collaboration with the line managers, is usually responsible for preparing job descriptions. The job description should include, at minimum, three sections.

1. First, there should be a paragraph on job duties, detailing day-to-day activities and responsibilities for the job. This can include such factors as the extent of independent judgment required, access to confidential information, the extent of supervision and direction received, the degree of internal and external contacts, equipment or machinery used and skills needed (such as computers and expertise in computer languages), physical environment (office, shop), amount of travel involved, and responsibility for the "bottom line."

2. The next section should spell out the education required for the job. This should include a minimum level of required education (college degree, graduate study) and any preferred college major and important requisite courses (accounting courses, for example). Some job descriptions may substitute related job experience: for example, a master's degree or four years' related work experience. Educational requirements must be directly related to specific job tasks, and everyone currently holding a particular job should have that minimal educational level.

3. The third section should cover the number of years of previous experience required for successful job performance.

Figure 2-1 shows a sample job description for the position of auditor (page 12).

In some situations, candidates for high-level positions may negotiate the specifics of the job description so that it is more in line with their experience and the activities that give them the most satisfaction. And some companies are quite willing to make such changes if it means being able to attract highly qualified individuals.

Behavior Specifications

Although most companies do not list behavior specifications, since they are so fundamental to the development of a sound selection program it is very important for interviewers to develop such a set of specifications.

The first step in doing so is for the interviewer to study the job description. The second step is to study the kinds of behaviors shown by people already doing the job in question, in an effort to determine

Examines and analyzes accounting records of the establishment and prepares reports concerning its financial status and operating procedures. Reviews data regarding material assets, net worth, liabilities, capital stock, surplus, income, and expenditures. Inspects items in books of original entry to determine if proper procedures in recording transactions were followed. Counts cash on hand and inspects notes receivable and payable, negotiable securities, and cancelled checks. Verifies journal and ledger entries of cash and check payments, purchases, expenses, and trial balances by examining and authenticating inventory. Reports to management concerning scope of audit, financial condition found, and sources and application of funds. May make recommendations regarding improvement of operations and financial condition of company. Works independently and usually travels to various divisions of the corporation. May supervise two to four assistants, but does not have "hire and fire" responsibility. Travel away from home base can average 40 to 60 percent of time worked. Long workdays (10 to 12 hours) toward the end of the fiscal year can be expected.

Requires college degree in finance or accounting with at least six courses in accounting as well as special training in auditing.

Requires at least two to three years' experience in a variety of accounting positions.

Figure 2-1. Sample job description for an auditor

unique experience, training, and specific skills required. This can be done by perusing application materials of people already doing the job, and then visiting the plant or office in order to observe the job in question and talk with the supervisor and individual workers. The behavior specification questionnaire shown in Figure 2-2 is a useful guide for organizing the desired material. Again using the auditor position as an example, Figure 2-3 shows what a properly and thoroughly assembled set of behavior specifications would look like.

A word of caution is in order. Items appearing on lists of behavior specifications should be regarded as *factors favorable to success* and

Position title _____

Interviewee _____

Location _____ Date _____

1. What kinds of aptitudes are required for this job?

Verbal _____

Quantitative _____

Mechanical _____

Clerical speed and accuracy _____

Other _____

2. Analytical ability. What interpretation, selection, and analysis are required for the job? To what extent do mental skills involve judgment and ingenuity? How complex are the problems to be solved?

_____

3. Employment training. *Once the employee is hired,* what training and experience are necessary for the average employee to become proficient in performing the job? How long does it take the average employee to absorb the training and experience? _____

_____

4. Responsibility for performance and materials. How closely is the employee supervised? What materials or machinery are involved?

_____

5. Responsibility for contacts. To what degree are poise, cooperation, and tact required in maintaining good working relationships? Is the employee required to communicate with co-workers only or with the general public as well, directly or by telephone? _____

_____

6. Responsibility for the direction of others. How many people does an incumbent in this job supervise? Does this person have disciplinary responsibility? _____

_____

Figure 2-2. Behavior specification questionnaire (continued on next page)

---

7. Working conditions. To what degree are there any disagreeable environmental factors? What about travel and long hours? ___

---

8. Critical personality traits needed. What are important traits of leadership, sales, sense of urgency in getting the job done, degree of maturity required? _____

---

9. Other required characteristics. _____

Figure 2-2. Behavior specification questionnaire (continued)

---

1. Required aptitudes.
   a. High degree of numerical aptitude.
   b. High degree of clerical speed and accuracy.
   c. Above average verbal ability.

2. Mental ability. High-level mental ability is required. This job involves a great amount of mathematical reasoning. Statistical data must be *interpreted* in the light of the facts and the company's needs. The auditor must be able to plan and organize and be able to see the broad picture. Financial statements and other reports have to be prepared for management—hence, the need for good verbal ability.

3. Employment training, once hired. The employee normally takes a six-month to one-year company-sponsored course in auditing practices and then spends at least one year as an assistant to an auditor in the field before being "turned loose" on his or her own.

4. Responsibility for performance and materials. Employee works independently on his or her own without a great amount of supervision. Must have excellent computer facility.

Figure 2-3. Sample of behavior specifications for auditor's position (continued on next page)

5. **Responsibility for contacts.** Auditors are often viewed as "investigators" by management whose books they are auditing. Hence, they are not always popular in a particular organization. For this reason, they should have an abundance of poise, tact, and an ability to establish rapport.

6. **Responsibility for the direction of others.** The auditor usually supervises two to four assistants but does not have disciplinary responsibility. This individual must have infectious enthusiasm for the work, which can rub off on the assistants and thus make the long hours less burdensome.

7. **Working conditions.** This job requires 40 to 60 percent travel and long hours toward the end of the fiscal year. Therefore, the employee needs a lot of energy and physical stamina as well as the ability to adjust to living away from home.

8. **Critical personality traits needed.** Because of the judgment factor involved and the access to confidential information, the employee must have a high degree of maturity and integrity. And, because the auditors have to face up to management and be willing to make confrontations when needed, they should be tough-minded.

9. **Other characteristics.** Because of the confinement of this work and the attention to detail needed, the better auditors tend to be slightly introverted and reflective.

Figure 2-3. Sample of behavior specifications for auditor's position (continued)

nothing more. These specifications represent a synthesized list of subjective opinions. And, valuable as these are, they cannot be quantified. For example, just because everyone involved has said that a given job requires superior mathematical ability, interviewers cannot insist that every successful applicant for that job score in the top 10 percent on a test of numerical ability. No candidate is expected to possess every single one of the favorable factors. But the point is that the more of these factors applicants have, the better qualified they are.

In developing behavior specifications, interviewers should concentrate first on those jobs that most frequently are filled by new hires, people from outside the company. As time permits, they can then develop specifications for those jobs they are less frequently called upon to fill.

Before embarking upon the task of developing behavior specifications, interviewers should look at a wide variety of jobs and keep in mind the qualifications needed for them, thus permitting them to be able to speak intelligently about given traits and their importance. If interviewers are able to give the impression of having some understanding of certain jobs, they will gain quicker rapport with supervisors and subordinates alike.

With these objectives in mind, we have prepared a series of general behavior specifications for a number of key higher-level jobs, based upon knowledge gained from evaluating candidates for these jobs over a period of many years. It should be emphasized that the specifications that follow are *general* rather than *specific*. Hence, they cannot be expected to represent the requirements for any one job in any given organization. On the contrary, they are designed to give the interviewer a general overview and to be used primarily as background information. Specific job demands vary widely from company to company, depending upon job content, organizational setup, and company atmosphere. Of course, in developing the following specifications, we have omitted certain common denominator traits that are important in practically all jobs, such as honesty, loyalty, willingness to work hard, and the ability to get along with others.

MANAGEMENT QUALIFICATIONS

Qualifications for executive positions vary with respect to level of responsibility and the kind of people to be supervised. The chief accountant, for example, need not have the same degree of dynamic, tough-minded leadership normally required in the plant superintendent. In general, however, the qualifications for the executive may be broken down into two categories: leadership and administrative ability.

Leadership	Administrative Ability
Assertiveness	High-level mental ability
Production-mindedness	Good verbal ability
Tough-mindedness	Good numerical ability
Self-confidence	Ability to think analytically and
Courage of convictions	critically
Ability to take charge	Good judgment
Ability to organize	Long-range planning ability
Decisiveness	Good cultural background
Ability to inspire others	
Depth and perspective	
Tact and social sensitivity	

The ideal executive is a happy blend of leader and administrator. As a leader, executives must be able to influence their subordinates to willingly carry out their wishes. They must also be forceful, dynamic, and willing to take charge. Since they are dealing with the human element, they must use tact and social sensitivity in their general approach. Social sensitivity, or awareness of the reactions of others, plays a big part in the development of good human relations. Leaders who understand their subordinates and sense their reactions know which ones need forceful direction and which ones need a pat on the back in order to obtain optimal job performance.

True leaders must be decisive, a trait born of self-confidence and courage of convictions. They must believe implicitly in their own abilities and, once they have set their course, they must follow through without any wavering of purpose. In this connection, too, they should be tough-minded, in the sense that they must be willing to make difficult decisions that may tread on the toes of a few but work for the good of the many. In the final analysis, industry rewards those who are able to get things accomplished. Thus, leaders must be able to organize and inspire their subordinates so that they accomplish their purpose in the shortest period of time.

As behind-the-scenes administrators, executives are faced with day-to-day as well as long-range planning. Since this is an intellectual function, it requires a rather high degree of mental ability. Executives are called upon to think in the abstract and to integrate a large number of complex factors. To do a top job as a manager, then, the individual's mental level should be appreciably above that of the average college graduate, including verbal and numerical abilities. High verbal ability allows a manager to clearly communicate, orally and on paper, which is a necessary trait since executives who cannot establish good lines of communications are handicapped indeed. Although numerical ability may not be quite as important as verbal ability in many executive positions, it nevertheless plays an important role in such functions as setting up budgets, analyzing statistical reports, and the like. And, with the increasing role of automation in the plant and office, managers without a fair amount of sophistication in quantitative analysis will be lost in the shuffle.

The administrator is constantly faced with the task of analyzing various problems and breaking them down into their component parts. In working out solutions to these problems, they cannot afford to take things at face value. They must examine each factor critically, looking beneath the surface to explore any hidden meaning. If they are to exercise good judgment, it logically follows that managers must have mental depth and perspective. Otherwise, they will find themselves in the position of not being able to see the forest for the trees.

Experience has shown that a good cultural background adds appreciably to one's ability to see the overall picture. Some knowledge of the arts and some understanding of the cultures of other people help one develop a body of knowledge that contributes to intellectual maturity and judgment. This is a factor to which many industrial leaders refer when they characterize someone as "broad-gauged."

The executive qualifications discussed above are, of course, not all-inclusive; there are obviously many other traits and abilities that make a contribution. We would like to emphasize again that no single executive is likely to possess all of the above qualifications. None of us is perfect; we all have some shortcomings. For the most part, we carry out our jobs as well as we do because certain of our assets are strong enough to compensate for our shortcomings. So it is with executives; they may possess certain traits in such abundance that they largely make up for what they lack in other areas.

RESEARCH AND DEVELOPMENT QUALIFICATIONS

Jobs in this category spread over a wide scale. At one end of the scale is the "blue sky" research worker who searches for truth for truth's sake. At the other end of the scale is the practical pilot-plant operator principally concerned with getting the "bugs" out of some process that others have conceived and developed. The vast majority of research and development people, however, fall somewhere between the two extremes. Their general qualifications can be summarized as follows:

Superior mental capacity	Creativity
Superior numerical ability	Carefulness
Good verbal ability	Methodicalness
Good mechanical comprehension	Ability to handle details
Ability to think analytically and critically	Patience
Tendency to be reflective	Good academic training

Intellectual Curiosity

There can be no substitute for top-level mental and mathematical abilities if one is to operate with a high degree of productiveness in a research and development job. In fact, this type of a position probably places more demands on intellect than any other industrial assignment. Much of the work involves thinking in the abstract and using current knowledge as a springboard to new and uncharted fields. In many technical jobs, moreover, mathematics and physics are requisite to obtaining the desired objectives. Thus, the best people invariably possess numerical facility as well as an understanding of mechanical principles. As a group, they are also remarkably analytical and critical in their thinking.

The ability to conceive new ideas is, of course, an important requirement for a research and development position. Here again, intellect plays an important part. Although not all brilliant people are necessarily creative, one seldom finds really creative people who do not have a high degree of intelligence. Such people are unusually reflective, in the sense that they have a strong theoretical drive. They have so much intellectual curiosity that they are motivated to dig to the bottom of a problem and find out what makes things tick. Their curiosity leads them to forsake the status quo in quest of new and better ways of doing things, a trait that can only bring more profound and positive change to the organization.

Because the job requires reflective individuals and those who can adjust to a somewhat confined work situation, research and development people usually display some degree of introversion. For the most part, they do not require contact with large numbers of people in order to find satisfaction on the job. On the contrary, they are usually content to work by themselves or as members of small groups.

Technical experiments are of such a precise nature that one minor slip may completely invalidate the results. Consequently, research and development people understand that their approach to problems must be carried out methodically, systematically, and with painfully accurate attention to detail. Nor can they afford to be impatient if their first hypothesis proves to be inadequate; the majority of new developments come only as a result of attacking a problem over and over again.

In view of the high technical demands and the unusual complexity of the work, extensive academic training is naturally an important prerequisite. Whether individuals aspire to work as chemists, chemical engineers, or mechanical engineers, they must have taken full advantage of their educational opportunities and acquired a tremendous body of knowledge and skills before they arrive on the industrial scene. Ordinarily, then, our top research and development people will have obtained high academic grades in college and in graduate school, and many of them will have earned Ph.D.s in their chosen fields.

PRODUCTION SUPERVISION QUALIFICATIONS

The people who oversee the manufacture of the final product include supervisors, general supervisors, and plant superintendents. Job requirements will vary with respect to the level of responsibility. The differences between supervisors and plant superintendents are those of degree rather than kind, however. We expect plant superintendents to have a higher degree of the essential qualifications than those possessed by general supervisors, which is, presumably, why they have been promoted to positions of more responsibility. Experience has shown that the following qualifications are generally basic for production supervision:

Good mental ability	Production-mindedness
Good verbal ability	Ability to improvise
Good numerical ability	Assertiveness
Good mechanical	Tough-mindedness
comprehension	Ability to see the overall picture
Self-confidence	Tact
Ability to plan	Strong practical interests
and organize	Social sensitivity

Production supervisors are a special breed. They are the people who devote most of their attention to putting out day-to-day fires and eliminating production bottlenecks. It is their prime function to get the final product "out the door." Consequently, they must have exceedingly strong practical interests and must be unusually production-minded. Supervisors, general supervisors, or plant superintendents who are not highly motivated to get things done in a hurry are not worth their salt. Since production bottlenecks may occur in the most unexpected places, production people must be good improvisers, individuals who can solve problems for which there has been little time to prepare. On the basis of their ingenuity and past experience, they must somehow make things work for the moment, even though a better solution to the problem may subsequently be found.

Anyone who is called upon to solve problems must, of course, have a fair amount of mental ability. Because the production supervisor's job requires so much ability to communicate with others, verbal ability is an important requisite, along with numerical ability. A certain degree of math facility is involved in such job functions as scheduling, preparing time sheets, and analyzing statistical reports. Here, too, the ever-increasing introduction of robots into the manufacturing process places a premium on quantitative analysis. More often than not, the manufacturing process has to do with making "hardware," objects such as appliances, airplanes, automobiles, and furnishings, and such activities also require mechanical know-how and understanding.

Although production supervisors are first and foremost leaders, they must also have some traits of the administrator in their makeup. They are faced with the problem of planning and organizing their work and must be able to see the broad picture. If they give an inordinate amount of attention to only one specific aspect of the work, the manufacturing process as a whole will suffer.

This type of work places unusually heavy demands on the leadership function. Production supervisors must have qualities that enable them to inspire their people, motivating them to carry out high-quality production in the shortest period of time possible. Confronted with the task of supervising some employees who may be hard to handle, supervisors must be particularly tough-minded, assertive, and self-confident. At the same time they cannot afford to ride roughshod over their subordinates. Tact and social sensitivity are important here, not only in dealing with subordinates, but in dealing with unions as well.

SALES QUALIFICATIONS

There is perhaps more variation in sales jobs than in any other single business function. Sales jobs range all the way from high-pressure, foot-in-the-door selling to low-pressure, technical sales service. Hence, some of the traits listed below will be more important in some sales jobs than in others. However, all salespeople have two important functions in common: they are required to contact people, and they are called upon to persuade others to their point of view. These functions inevitably demand the following qualifications:

Good verbal ability	Strong desire to make money
Good self-expression	Assertiveness
Extroversion	Tough-mindedness
Infectious enthusiasm	Self-confidence
Sense of humor	Tact

Persuasiveness   Social sensitivity
Practical interests   Self-discipline
Perseverance

The best salespeople are those who need the stimulation that comes from dealing with people. Quite the opposite of the reflective individual, they are likely to be extroverted, assertive, colorful, and infectiously enthusiastic. They call upon these traits in their efforts to persuade others to buy their product.

Competition being what it is, the sales job is not an easy one. The best salespersons are highly articulate, possess good basic verbal ability, and know how to handle themselves adroitly in face-to-face situations. The last ability, of course, involves tact and social sensitivity. Salespeople must know when to talk and when to keep still and must be continually alert to the customer's reactions. This permits them to take a different tack if they note that their first approach is not getting across. A good sense of humor is indispensable in many types of sales jobs.

A salesperson's lot can be arduous. Often, they live out of suitcases and spend days at a time on the road away from their families. There must be some motivation, then, that attracts them to this field, in addition to the one of having a chance to deal with people. That motivation is usually compensation.

Most salespeople are extremely practical and have a strong desire to make money. Because many salespeople are paid on a commission basis, and because sales jobs as a whole pay better than many other types of work, the better salespeople find that they can make more money in sales than in any other type of work for which they might qualify.

The task of getting a hearing from a potential customer demands certain traits of personality. Busy executives often feel they do not have time to see the salesperson and instruct their secretaries accordingly. To get past this obstacle, then, salespeople must be unobtrusively assertive and self-confident. They must be sufficiently tough-minded to take rebuffs in stride.

Many salespeople work largely on their own, with very little supervision from their immediate superiors. This calls for a good bit of self-discipline. The ones who go to the movies in the afternoon just because they have made a big sale during the morning seldom turn out to be top producers. They must be constantly aware of the law of averages, that the more calls they make the more sales they are likely to get. In going after big accounts, moreover, they cannot become discouraged. They must persevere, calling on the account again and again until they finally make the sale.

FINANCE QUALIFICATIONS

This category includes a series of jobs ranging from the accounting clerk to the company comptroller. Again, although there is a marked similarity in the traits required in all these jobs, the degree of each trait required will vary in accordance with the level of responsibility. The lower-level jobs, of course, do not make as much demand on the intellectual and administrative factors. In practically all financial jobs, however, the following traits and abilities play an important role:

High-level mental ability	Good judgment
High-level numerical ability	Ability to see the
Good verbal ability	overall picture
Carefulness	Methodicalness
Good clerical aptitude	Orderliness
Ability to think analytically	Introversion
and critically	Attention to detail
Ability to plan and organize	

Although employees in the financial field do deal with people, they are principally concerned with figures and with things. Their work is likely to be rather confining, and the people who adjust most easily to this type of work are, therefore, inclined to be somewhat introverted. Since even the smallest error must be found before reports are submitted, financial people place great stress on accuracy and close attention to detail. As a group, they are very careful, methodical, and systematic.

High-level intelligence and superior numerical facility are prime requisites in financial jobs. Arithmetical computation is not in itself sufficient. Practically all of these jobs require a high degree of mathematical reasoning. Statistical data must be *interpreted* in light of the facts and in light of the company's needs. Clerical detail must be handled quickly and accurately. This is why the better people in these fields have high clerical aptitude. And at some point, financial statements and other reports have to be prepared for top management, so a degree of verbal ability is also necessary.

At the upper levels, finance people are required to supervise relatively large groups of workers. Since the majority of their subordinates are likely to be somewhat introverted, however, supervisors are normally not required to exert dynamic, tough-minded leadership. Rather, the leadership needed is of an administrative character. Principal emphasis here is placed upon good judgment, ability to plan and organize, and ability to see the broad picture. Comptrollers must be able to watch all the company operations and must be able to assimilate and integrate their findings so that they can keep their fingers on the financial pulse of the entire enterprise. Above all, they must be analytical and critical. Comptrollers must take nothing for granted; they are accountable to top management and therefore must not only be in possession of the facts but also be aware of the underlying reasons.

EMPLOYEE RELATIONS QUALIFICATIONS

There was a time when little thought was given to the demands of employee relations work. For this reason, human resources staffs in many companies were not carefully selected or trained in their specialty. Nor were these people given the chance to develop the skills with which to do their jobs—at least to the same degree as personnel in other jobs.

Thankfully, however, that situation has changed. The field of employee relations has finally emerged as a profession. This happy development is due primarily to the fact that labor unions and management have finally awakened to the need to stimulate the growth and development of all personnel. Because their tactics have been so effective, labor unions have literally forced management to staff human resources departments with more competent people, men and women who can meet with labor leaders on an equal footing.

After many years of neglecting the human element in an industry, management has at long last discovered that its workforce represents its greatest single asset. Today, many progressive organizations sponsor comprehensive programs designed to help each individual within the company realize his or her greatest potential. These programs include more effective selection and placement procedures, better-designed merit-rating procedures, and a wide variety of employee-training procedures. Such activities obviously require capable people at the helm.

The employee relations function, as it now exists in more progressive organizations, may be divided into two categories: human resources and labor relations. As might be expected in view of the differences between these two functions, the qualifications necessary for success in the human resources end of the business vary somewhat from those required in labor relations work. There are many individuals capable of doing an excellent job in human resources (which includes recruiting, selection, placement, wage and salary evaluation, employee benefits, and training) who are completely incapable of bargaining with unions. The best-qualified employee relations person, of course, will possess qualifications for both types of jobs. These are the people who have the best chance eventually of heading up the employee relations department. In order to clarify the difference between the two major employee relations functions, requisite traits are listed separately below:

Human Resources	**Labor Relations**
Good mental ability	Good mental ability
Good verbal ability	Good verbal ability
Good self-expression	Good self-expression
Ability to think analytically and critically	Ability to think analytically and critically
Good judgment	Good judgment
Ability to plan and organize	Shrewdness
Social drive (desire to help others)	Assertiveness
	Tough-mindedness
Genuine liking for people	Courage of one's convictions
Extroversion	Self-confidence

Human Resources	Labor Relations
Friendliness	Fortitude
Warmth	Perseverance
Tact	Fair-mindedness
Social sensitivity	Ability to improvise

Many people are initially attracted to human resources because they have a genuine liking for people and are strongly motivated to help others. This is all for the good, because these qualities play an important part in such activities as placement, training, and employee benefits. Individuals who carry out these duties are usually extroverted, friendly, and the kind of people to whom others like to take their problems. To help others with their problems, a human resources employee must be able to approach individuals and win their confidence. This obviously takes an abundance of tact and social sensitivity. But people in human resources must not be so highly motivated to help others that they permit their hearts to run away with their heads.

Many of their duties—particularly that of employment interviewing—call for mature, objective decisions. Even though these decisions involve people rather than things or ideas, they should nonetheless be objective and impartial. Practically every human resources function involves the evaluation of people in one way or another. The job requires intelligence, judgment, and good powers of analysis. Human resources people work largely through the verbal medium, moreover, and should be able to speak well.

Although people in the labor relations field need many of the traits and abilities required by people in human resources, their job demands an additional group of personality characteristics. They have to deal with representatives of labor, many of whom are aggressive, tough, and able strategists. Labor negotiators have to be exceedingly strong-minded, so that they will be able to take it when the going gets rough. They must be self-confident and assertive and have the courage of their convictions. Good labor negotiators are also shrewd individuals, people who have a little of the "Yankee horse trader" in their makeup. At the same time, they must develop a reputation for being completely fair; otherwise they will never be able to win the confidence of labor representatives or develop a working relationship with them.

Bargaining sessions consume long, weary hours during which each side jockeys for position. Company representatives at the bargaining table must learn to meet fire with fire, match persistence with persistence, and maintain their position without getting discouraged. They also have to be good improvisers, in the sense that they can cope with unanticipated developments. All of this takes its toll on many individuals. As pointed out previously, there are numerous people in human resources who simply do not have the resilience and mental toughness required to succeed in labor relations.

MATCHING THE APPLICANT WITH THE JOB

We have discussed at length the need for acquiring a complete understanding of the jobs for which applicants are to be selected. Remember, though, that the behavior specifications outlined above, while not all-inclusive, nevertheless represent the *ideal* worker. In the appraisal of candidates, it is unlikely to find any one individual who possesses all the favorable factors for any given job. All of us have our shortcomings, and it has already been pointed out that the interview that brings to light no unfavorable information is a poor interview. Almost every candidate will therefore lack some of the desirable factors. But the best of these people will have assets in such abundance that they compensate for their liabilities. The interviewer's job, then, is to find the applicant who has the most desirable qualifications for a specific job.

At this point, it is only fair to ask the question, "How do we go about determining whether or not an applicant actually possesses the appropriate qualifications?" A few of these qualifications can be determined by means of aptitude tests, but tests are primarily useful in measuring *abilities alone*. It is necessary therefore to rely upon the interview as a means of appraising *personality, motivation, interests, character*, and *intellectual ability*.

Chapter Three | Preliminary Selection Steps

Since hiring interviews are a time-consuming and hence relatively expensive procedure, they should be used only with those candidates who satisfy the minimum job requirements. This is why progressive companies use a series of screening techniques designed to quickly eliminate those applicants whose qualifications are inappropriate. Such devices, when properly used, are of value to the candidate as well as to the company, since the overall hiring procedure normally consumes several hours, and candidates should not be asked to waste their time being processed for jobs they have little chance of obtaining. An employment setup that does not allow for reasonably quick screening is not only inefficient for the company, but also unfair to job-seekers.

The selection of higher-level people in many companies is often even more ineffective, usually consisting of a whole series of interviews with department heads and other key people. Since most such people have not been trained in the techniques of developing information and interpreting it correctly, the results are often far from what they should be. In any panel of five individuals, there may be one or two keen observers of human nature, persons who can make a good employment decision. But others who base their decisions on hunch alone frequently override their votes. In fact, many line managers, whether they realize it or not, advocate hiring individuals with personality traits similar to their own. In addition, panel interviewing is often an ordeal for higher-level applicants. They are subjected to a daylong experience during which they are usually asked the same questions over and over again. This is not only hard on the applicant but also bad for the company image.

In companies where interviewers have been trained, there is only one evaluation interview. If the decision in that interview is negative, no further interviews are scheduled, and the unsuccessful applicant is assigned to a person of lower rank, who provides a tour of the company for public relations purposes. This is a great time saver for important people who would normally participate in a panel interview, and it can actually save thousands of dollars over a period of a year.

Several years ago, one of the authors was asked to review selection procedures for hiring college graduates in a very large company. At the outset, he was told that this technically oriented company placed high value on hiring the best-qualified new people, and that each of five top managers spent at least one hour interviewing every single candidate. In that year, they had each interviewed 196 candidates and selected a total of 27.

By placing a dollar figure on the value of one hour's time for managers at the top level, multiplying that by five and again by 196, we determined that the company was spending well over $150,000 per year on a selection program that produced less than 30 people—and not doing a very good job of it at that! This is a classic example of the extent to which an inefficient selection program can waste the valuable time of highly placed people. By training interviewers to do a much better job of preliminary selection on the college campuses, using aptitude tests, and training human resources people to conduct evaluation interviews, only a fraction of the initial population of candidates was subsequently referred to the five top managers—all of whom expressed astonishment at the greatly improved caliber of the people they were now seeing.

When the evaluation interviewer's decision is positive, applicants are then scheduled with other people in the organization, whose purpose may be to check qualifications and sell the applicant on the company. Frequently, this person is the line manager and/or the person for whom they will be working. Further interviews may involve other important individuals in the organization.

Companies with well-organized human resources departments utilize a number of screening devices, such as an application form, a preliminary interview, aptitude tests, and reference checks. As important as these steps are, however, at some point the all-important hiring decision must be made, and that normally occurs at the end of the final interview, which represents the solid core of any good selection program.

The early selection steps, then, have two functions: (1) to eliminate those applicants whose qualifications are obviously inappropriate, and (2) to provide information that will be helpful to the interviewer at the time of the final decision. In effect, these selection steps represent a series of screens through which the successful applicant must pass, each screen being constructed of finer mesh than the previous one, so that only the most appropriately qualified candidates will survive. The final interviewer sees only a fraction of the number of people who apply for jobs and is thus able to spend as much time as needed with each surviving candidate.

Despite the fact that this book is primarily concerned with interviewing techniques, some discussion of preliminary selection devices helps to place the interview in proper perspective.

RECRUITING

No hiring program can be effective unless the number of applicants for a given type of work is substantially greater than the number of jobs to be filled. The very word "selection" implies the choice, for any given task, of the one best-qualified individual from among a number of available candidates. Wherever careful selection is applied, it is of paramount importance that there be a relatively large reservoir of candidates from which the final selectees are chosen. This is what is known as the *selection ratio*. Ordinarily this ratio should be at least five or six candidates for each person finally selected.

The law of supply and demand always operates insofar as the labor population is concerned, and the available pool of candidates for jobs requiring highly developed skills and long years of training is always limited. At the same time, it is important to choose the best people obtainable. In times of great economic activity, many companies take a defeatist attitude toward the recruiting problem. They give up too easily, without having tapped all possible sources of supply. Too often, they settle for a "warm body."

More alert organizations maintain an aggressive recruiting policy. This is especially important today in order to find and hire qualified minorities. With this in mind, some companies contact minority clubs and other organizations as a part of their recruiting program. Some companies pay a premium to any current employee who personally recruits people who are eventually hired. And many organizations hire students for summer jobs at the end of their junior year. This not only provides a firsthand impression of the student's worth but also weighs heavily in that student's eventual employment decision once college has been completed.

APPLICATION FORM

The application form represents such an important initial screening device that most companies would do well to critically examine their own forms. Are they up-to-date in the sense that they do not ask for information that is currently illegal, such as an applicant's specific age, marital status, or number of dependents? Do they provide space for coded information concerning sex and age, as a means of monitoring the applicant flow and insuring the selection of a sufficient number of minorities and females? Do they provide space for an applicant's likes and dislikes at various jobs and best and least liked subjects in school?

Since as many as 50 percent of all applicants for lower-level jobs—and a high percentage of applicants for higher-level jobs as well—can be eliminated on the basis of application data alone, the application form should obviously contain as much information as possible. As noted earlier in this chapter, the elimination of a sizable number of applicants at this first stage of selection means that final interviewers will be required to see fewer people and will be able to spend more time with the people they do see.

Job descriptions and behavior specifications represent the key to the proper elimination of applicants on the basis of the application form. Thus, if the specifications indicate a minimum number of years of specific experience or education, application forms can be quickly scanned to determine those individuals who satisfy the requirements as well as those who do not. The latter can of course be screened out at this time.

If, in the interest of hiring people with good job stability, a company has the requirement in writing that it will not hire individuals with more than two jobs during the past five years, additional candidates can be eliminated on that basis. Gaps in dates of employment—except in the case of people returning to the work force after raising children or serving as caregivers to aged parents—raise further questions. If such gaps cannot be satisfactorily accounted for in the subsequent preliminary interview, some people may be eliminated on that basis. Failure to move ahead or to achieve reasonable increases in pay over a period of time raises still further questions, which must also be discussed in the preliminary interview.

When specifications prescribe a fair degree of mathematical facility, persons who least liked "number crunching" on previous jobs and least liked mathematics in high school or college would not seem to represent a good "fit" for the job in question. However, if all other aspects of a person's history seem suitable, such an individual might be passed on to the employment test stage in order to determine just how much mathematical aptitude he or she possesses. Finally, if a job requires shift work and if an applicant indicates distaste for shift work or a flat refusal to do it, elimination becomes automatic.

THE PRELIMINARY INTERVIEW

The preliminary interview has three primary functions: (1) to make certain that the applicant has answered all questions on the application form, (2) to *screen out* candidates who are obviously unqualified for the job or jobs in question, and (3) to provide information for the final interviewer on those applicants who have been *screened in*. Because important decisions must be made within a short period of time—usually five to 10 minutes—the preliminary interviewer should be well trained and exceedingly perceptive.

Preliminary interviewers usually use the completed application as the basis for their brief discussion with applicants. If a previous job appears to have some relevance to the job for which the candidate is applying, the interviewer may ask for a more complete description of that experience. If an individual's education or background appears limited, the interviewer may ask about any additional schooling, such as nondegree courses taken at community colleges, on-line or correspondence courses, on-the-job training, or military service.

It is a matter of common sense that only those candidates who are obviously unqualified should be screened out by means of the application and preliminary interview. Doubtful cases should be screened in, thus giving the individual an opportunity to take the employment test and perhaps to participate in the final interview. This is particularly true in the case of minorities and females, where affirmative action goals must be kept in mind. It is conceivable that final interviewers, with more time to explore an individual's history, may be able to discover some compensating asset for what appears to be a somewhat serious shortcoming. However, this is not to say that employment standards should vary with respect to sex or race. In the final analysis, employment standards should be the same for men and women, and for minorities and nonminorities alike.

Perceptive preliminary interviewers can frequently uncover information that should be followed up on in the final interview. Such information should, of course, be written down and passed along to whoever makes the final decision. For example, the preliminary interviewer may discover that a given individual left a certain job before obtaining the next position. Although this normally reflects poor judgment and some degree of immaturity, it would normally be insufficient to eliminate that person from further consideration. At the same time, it could represent valuable input for the final interviewer. Or, the preliminary interviewer may get the feeling that an applicant is not telling the truth, but because of lack of sufficient time may not be able to document this sufficiently, and, accordingly, passes on these impressions for further investigation by the final interviewer.

APTITUDE TESTS

Aptitude tests should be an important preliminary selection step, but they have largely disappeared from the employment scene. So many charges of discrimination have been leveled at these tests since the enactment of the Civil Rights Act that most companies now believe it is illegal to use any kind of employment test. However, this is not the case at all. A careful reading of the Equal Employment Opportunity Commission Guidelines reveals that aptitude and dexterity tests may still be used *providing they have been statistically validated, in the sense that a positive relationship can be shown between the test scores and success on the jobs for which the tests are being used as a predictor.* The Civil Rights Act, then, does not state that tests cannot be used; it simply requires that any test utilized in the selection program must have been appropriately *validated.*

Since far too many companies were using aptitude tests without any knowledge as to whether or not such tests were making any positive contribution, the Civil Rights Act has had a positive effect. It is only unfortunate that so many companies have eliminated the use of tests entirely rather than to undertake validation studies. Actually, aptitude tests have a long history of reliability in measuring such factors as mental ability, verbal ability, numerical ability, mechanical aptitude, and clerical aptitude, as well as manual and digital dexterity. Such tests can provide far more valid results than can be obtained by means of the interview, no matter how well trained the interviewer may be. Every effort should therefore be made to restore tests to their rightful place in the selection program.

Although most companies do not have the expertise to develop and validate their own tests, there are many reputable consulting organiza-

tions that specialize in this function. Companies desiring to restore aptitude tests to their selection programs should retain the services of a
knowledgeable consultant to help them with this phase of their program.

REFERENCE CHECK

Ideally, it would be preferable to check references prior to the final interview, so that discrepancies between application data and the reference check could be discussed at that time. In most cases, however,
this is impractical, because the return of reference information usually takes several days or even weeks. As a consequence, it is more practical to complete the final interview and then run reference checks on
only those who have survived that final stage of the selection process.

Human resources people know that reference checks have their
limitations. Some previous employers fail to respond, and those who do
respond are often reluctant to report any negative information.
Therefore, it is best to request only factual information such as dates of
employment, positions held, reasons for leaving, and attendance record.
Reference checks are usually run on only the last five years of employment; attendance records are usually limited to the past two years.

Reference checks should be made only by mail as people usually
will not respond to such requests over the phone. In large corporations,
it may not be possible to run a check on every single person to be hired.
In that case, the company will check perhaps one out of three or one
out of five, making certain that on a percentage basis it processes an
equal percentage of white males, females, and minority applicants.

DISCREPANCIES

In cases where there is a substantial discrepancy between application
information and the reference check—or where information of a derogatory nature is returned to the company by a previous employer—applicants must be given an opportunity to present their side of the story.
If the discrepancy is sufficiently serious and if the applicant fails to
convince the interviewer of his or her honesty, the applicant is normally turned down for employment. If that person has already been

employed, he or she will usually be terminated. In all fairness, though, such an applicant must be given a hearing.

PRELIMINARY SELECTION STEPS PROVIDE VALUABLE LEADS FOR THE FINAL INTERVIEW

Throughout the whole process, there should be open lines of communication between those who carry out the preliminary selection steps and the final interviewer. The preliminary interviewer frequently develops inconclusive information that should be passed on to the final interviewer. The person who administers the company's aptitude test can make valuable observations that also should be passed along. That person may notice that an applicant "jumps the gun," beginning the test before the starting signal has actually been given and continuing to work after the stopping signal has been indicated. Such behavior might represent a possible clue to dishonesty in certain situations, or might indicate that the applicant has a strong need to be competitive. Forewarned, the final interviewer is therefore in a position to follow up in an area that might have otherwise escaped attention.

Having discussed the preliminary steps of the selection program, we are now ready to take up the final step—the final interview. This is discussed in the next part, *Interviewing Tactics*.

Part Two | Interviewing Tactics

Chapter Four | The Strategy Behind the Evaluation Interview

I nterviewers are faced with two broad objectives: they must be able to develop relevant information, and they must be able to interpret the information they bring to light. In earlier chapters we have referred to the final or evaluation interview as the most important selection procedure. This is because it is here that all information obtained from the application form, the preliminary interview, the aptitude tests, and the reference check is integrated with other factors of the individual's background and the final decision is made.

Candidates who have made it to this point obviously have something to offer. They have passed many employment tests, they have demonstrated some stability in their employment history, and their previous work history and educational background reflect some degree of relevance in terms of the jobs for which they are being considered. But there are still very important questions about these individuals that have not yet been answered. Up to this point, we do not know how diligently they will be willing to work, whether they are likely to get along well with people, whether they can adapt to the work environment, whether they can solve complex problems, or whether they have potential for leadership. It is to these important areas that we address ourselves in the final interview.

Essential Aspects of the Final Interview

We have commented earlier that a vast majority of interviewers are "turned loose" in their jobs without any formal training at all. As a consequence, they may not have a plan and, hence, do not use their time effectively. Many do far too much of the talking themselves, and many, perhaps unconsciously, base their final decision on surface impressions, because they do not know how to probe for relevant, hard data.

In the kind of interview described here, we *do* operate according to plan (see the Interview Guide in the Appendix). We take candidates back to their earlier work experience and proceed chronologically through all their jobs up to their present position or last job. From there we discuss educational background, starting with high school and proceeding to college and graduate school. During this discussion, we probe for clues to behavior in an effort to get a clear picture of strengths and weaknesses.

This is the type of interview, moreover, where the candidate has center stage and is encouraged to do most of the talking. Interviewers develop such a high degree of rapport that candidates talk spontaneously and usually provide a clear picture of who they are and what they are like deep down inside. In such an interview, interviewers usually find it necessary to talk only about 15 percent of the time. This gives them a first-rate opportunity to sit back and analyze clues to behavior as they are reflected in the candidate's spontaneous remarks.

Unlike interviewers who base their hiring decisions on hunches or surface impressions, we make every effort to document our findings with concrete data drawn from the candidate's history. Thus, a finding such as *willingness to work* should be based upon such evidence as beginning work as an adolescent, long hours spent on certain jobs, "moonlighting" (working on two or more jobs at the same time), or carrying out a substantial (20 hours a week or more) part-time job while carrying a full academic load in school.

Evaluating Past Behavior Patterns

Experience has shown that the best way to predict what a person will do in the future is based on what he or she has done in the past.

Although it is possible for individuals to grow and develop, and in that way to modify their behavior, few people are likely to overcome completely the effect that long years of behaving in a certain manner has produced in them. Just as this is true for negative behavior, so it is also true that positive past behaviors can predict future job performance.

For example, if a woman has worked hard all her life from the time she was a teenager, she is very likely to work hard for her new employer. And if a man has shown the ability to adapt to new and changing situations in his previous job experiences, he is more likely to be able to make whatever adjustments may be required in the new job for which he is being considered. Moreover, if the candidate has been able to stay with most of her previous jobs for a reasonable period of time—three to five years—she is quite likely to remain with her new employer for a similar period. Finally, if candidates have demonstrated the ability to get along with people on previous jobs, in extracurricular activities in school, or in activities outside of work or school, they are very likely to get along well with people in their new workplace.

Evaluating Experience, Training, and Intelligence

In addition to the integration of all information obtained from previous selection steps, it becomes the function of the interviewer to (1) determine the relevance of a candidate's experience and training in terms of the demands of a specific job, (2) appraise his or her personality, motivation, and character, and (3) in the absence of aptitude tests, evaluate mental ability.

The third factor—mental ability—is of particular importance in selecting people for higher-level jobs. Most companies prefer to hire individuals with potential for advancement, and here intelligence plays a key role. Other factors being equal, the extent to which an individual is capable of promotion to more complex and demanding jobs is frequently determined by the amount of intelligence he or she possesses. Suggestions for making these determinations appear in later chapters of this book.

Once all these factors have been assessed, the interviewer is in a position to make the final hiring decision. This is of necessity a subjective decision, based upon the interviewer's experience, judgment, and training. Nevertheless, it should be based on factual evidence rather than an unsupported hunch. In the final analysis, interviewers not only evaluate a candidate's assets and liabilities in terms of the demands of a given job, they must also judge the extent to which the assets outweigh the liabilities, or vice versa. Only in this way can they rate candidates as excellent, above average, average, below average, or poor.

Since most candidates approach the interview with the objective of putting their best foot forward, the interviewer must be motivated from the very beginning to search for unfavorable information, in order to avoid being taken in by surface appearances and behavior. Interviewers are human and thus, despite their efforts to maintain objectivity, they react more favorably to some persons than to others. When the initial reaction is favorable, the interviewer has a natural tendency to look only for those clues that will confirm the original impression. This becomes a problem, because *the interview that results in no unfavorable information is inescapably a poor interview.*

Actually, a good interview is an exercise in indirection. By means of appropriate suggestions, comments, and questions, we try to elicit spontaneous information without having to ask direct or pointed questions. Obviously, if we are unable to get the desired information by means of indirection, our questions must gradually become more direct. Even so, we try to soften such questions by the use of appropriately worded introductory phrases and qualifying adjectives. Specific techniques for accomplishing this objective will be found in a later chapter.

Playing Down Unfavorable Information

Just as we compliment candidates on their achievements, so should we *play down* their problems or difficulties. This is done to make it easier for individuals to talk about negative aspects of their backgrounds, and since we are searching for shortcomings as well as assets, this becomes an important part of the interview technique.

Playing down takes the form of some casual, understanding remark. If, for example, a candidate talks about the "terrible time she had with mathematics in school," this can be played down by such a sympathetic remark as "All of us have different aptitudes; the chances are that you may have been a lot stronger in the verbal area." Or, if a candidate admits to a lack of self-confidence, the interviewer might say, "Self-confidence is a trait that most people develop as a result of living a little longer and acquiring more experience."

When candidates discuss unfavorable information of a more serious nature, such as poor attendance on a previous job or a fiery temper, a casual, sympathetic remark on the part of the interviewer would *not* be appropriate. In such a case, it is better to compliment the individual for being able to recognize the problem and face up to it. An appropriate comment might be "The fact that you are aware of this situation and have been able to face up to it means that you have already taken the first step toward doing something about it." Such a statement by no means makes light of the individual's problem but does acknowledge being able to face up to it, and this is usually enough to make a person feel better about having revealed the difficulty.

No matter what, *interviewers should never tell candidates anything that is untrue.* If a person should admit to a lack of initiative, for example, it would be inappropriate to say, "Oh, that is something you should be able to overcome very easily." Since traits of this kind tend to become quite deeply imbedded in the personality structure, they are *not* easily overcome. Most candidates would be aware of this and hence would detect the ring of insincerity in an interviewer's comment.

However, the interviewer who gives the slightest indication that judgment is being adversely influenced by unfavorable information will get no further information of this kind. Once interviewers react negatively—either verbally or facially—they disqualify themselves as sympathetic listeners. No one willingly and spontaneously talks about difficulties and failures in a climate where the listener does not give the appearance of being understanding. On the other hand, when such information is not only accepted without surprise or disapproval but also played down, the candidate is permitted to *save face* and usually finds it easier to discuss additional negative data if this should be part of his or her history.

WHAT THE GOVERNMENT SAYS

According to the Equal Employment Opportunity Commission (EEOC), the Age Discrimination in Employment Act (ADEA) specifically prohibits age discrimination in hiring practices including:

1. "Statements or specifications in job notices or advertisements of age preference and limitations. An age limit may only be specified in the rare circumstance where age has been proven to be a bona fide occupational qualification (BFOQ).

2. "Discrimination on the basis of age by apprenticeship programs, including joint labor-management apprenticeship programs; and denial of benefits to older employees. An employer may reduce benefits based on age only if the cost of providing the reduced benefits to older workers is the same as the cost of providing benefits to younger workers.

3. "Before making an offer of employment, an employer may not ask job applicants about the existence, nature, or severity of a disability. Applicants may be asked about their ability to perform job functions. A job offer may be conditioned on the results of a medical examination, but only if the examination is required for all entering employees in the same job category. Medical examinations of employees must be job-related and consistent with business necessity.

4. "It is illegal to discriminate against an individual because of birthplace, ancestry, culture, or linguistic characteristics common to a specific ethnic group. A rule requiring that employees speak only English on the job may violate Title VII unless an employer shows that the requirement is necessary for conducting business. If the employer believes such a rule is necessary, employees must be informed when English is required and the consequences for violating the rule.

5. "Title VII prohibits discrimination because of participation in schools or places of worship associated with a particular racial, ethnic, or religious group as well as denying employment oppor-

tunities because of marriage to, or association with, an individual of a particular race, religion, national origin, or an individual with a disability.

6. "Title VII's broad prohibitions against sex discrimination specifically cover:

   - **Sexual Harassment**—This includes practices ranging from direct requests for sexual favors to workplace conditions that create a hostile environment for persons of either gender, including same sex harassment. (The "hostile environment" standard also applies to harassment on the basis of race, color, national origin, religion, age, and disability.)
   - **Pregnancy Based Discrimination**—Pregnancy, childbirth, and related medical conditions must be treated in the same way as other temporary illnesses or conditions."

While asking questions during an interview regarding the applicant's sex, age, race, and marital status is prohibited, there are, however, instances where it is appropriate, for example, to ask a relationship-related question. For example, if the applicant is a single mother, it is appropriate to ask how she plans to handle child care, because that has a direct impact on her job.

Interviewers do have the right to determine how well candidates have performed in their previous jobs or in school. This is obviously work-related because it provides strong clues concerning an individual's ability to handle a job for which he or she is being considered. If there is consistency of performance on previous jobs, that will probably continue in the new job.

A good rule of thumb when posing questions is this: put yourself in the applicant's place. If the question were something you feel would infringe on your own personal sense of privacy and being, then don't ask it. What we have found is that, at the end of the day, common sense and common decency are the best rules.

Chapter Five | Developing Rapport

In an effort to help candidates open up and tell their entire story, we introduce a number of techniques here, which have been clinically tested over the years. If these techniques are used successfully, candidates gradually develop confidence in the interviewer. They begin to realize it is to their advantage to disclose not only their assets, but also those areas that need further improvement, thus becoming partners in the interview. Now they assume center stage and spontaneously discuss their life stories.

Unfortunately, in too many interviews, the so-called *question-and-answer technique* prevails. In such an interview, the interviewer asks the questions, and the candidate answers the questions and waits for the next one. This type of interview is not only stilted and mechanical but, more seriously, gives candidates an opportunity to screen their replies. Thus, they're inclined to provide responses they think will put them in the best light, rather than tell the story as it actually is. Moreover, interviewers do almost half the talking, leaving candidates with much less opportunity to discuss all the relevant aspects of their background.

The question-and-answer approach to interviewing also tends to take on the aspects of an inquisition. Candidates feel they are being pulled and hence are uncomfortable. As a consequence, they often provide as little information about themselves as possible and almost never discuss any of their shortcomings. The goal here is not to put candidates on the spot. Rather, the interviewer should try to develop a harmonious relationship, one in which candidates not only feel comfortable, but also develop so much trust in the interviewer that they begin to talk spontaneously. When this happens, instead of waiting for the next question, they tend to discuss their background with appropriate elaboration, to the extent that their discourse becomes natural and unconstrained.

When people talk spontaneously, information seems to well up and bubble out in such a way that there is no need or, indeed, opportunity to screen their replies. Hence, spontaneous information is much more likely to reflect an individual's true feelings, needs, or anxieties, and more often than not, spontaneous information contains clues to shortcomings. Remember that interviewers must search for candidates' shortcomings as well as their assets. Otherwise, it is not only impossible to make appropriate job placements, but individuals may be hired for job situations in which they would be incompetent and conceivably quite miserable.

Interviewers who take the time to acquire proficiency with these techniques will discover that they have a completely new tool at their disposal, which will not only help them in the interview, but will also come to their assistance in many other aspects of their lives. People who have learned how to develop rapport become better supervisors, do a better job of feeding back appraisal information, and even become more popular at social gatherings.

SMALL TALK

In any conversation between two people, it is only natural to begin with some pleasantry rather than to delve directly into the purpose of the meeting. As far as the interviewer is concerned, this becomes an important aspect of establishing initial rapport. This is the interviewer's first opportunity to get candidates to assume a major portion of the conversational load. If they can be helped to do most of the talking during this early phase of the interview, they naturally assume this to be their role throughout and often fall into this role without any difficulty at all. However, if the small talk revolves around a series of short, direct questions, such as "How was your trip?" it usually leads to a question-and-answer approach where the interviewer does as much as half the talking. In that case, candidates have the right to assume that their role is one of simply answering any question that may be addressed to them rather than talking spontaneously.

The Importance of Beginning Small Talk with a General Question

Rather than pose questions that invite short, yes or no responses, it is more desirable to use a general "pump-priming" question—one that cannot be answered without a fair amount of discussion. Such questions require preparation, however, and cannot be expected to be phrased on the spur of the moment. Prior to the interview, the interviewer should study the completed application, in an effort to come up with one or two topics on which the candidate might be expected to talk freely and perhaps enthusiastically. Such topics might be concerned with a particular interest, some hobby or sport the individual participates in, some indicated achievement such as a scholarship, or perhaps differences encountered living in two different parts of the country. Whatever the topic, the initial question should be broad enough in nature so that the candidate will be required to talk two or three minutes in order to answer it. Several examples of such pump-priming questions are listed below.

1. "I notice from your application that you like to ski. Tell me, how did you get involved in skiing? Where do you most like to ski? What kind of satisfaction do you get out of it?"

2. "In looking over your application, I noticed that you were given an award at the Ford Motor Company for making a valuable suggestion concerning your work. Tell me, what did the award involve? What did the suggestion accomplish?"

3. "I notice from your application that you have worked in Silicon Valley as well as here in the Midwest. How do the two areas of the country compare with respect to things like climate, cost of living, recreational opportunities, attitude of the people, that sort of thing?"

Questions such as those listed above are sufficiently complex that it usually requires some time to answer them. If the candidate stops after a sentence or two, simply wait, drawing upon the technique to be discussed later—the calculated pause. In posing any incidental question designed to promote small talk, interviewers should make an effort to be as pleasant as possible, treating the subject as what it actually is, an "icebreaker," rather than a more serious part of the interview.

As long as the candidate keeps talking, interviewers should not take any part in the discussion at all. They should simply smile, nod their heads, and engage in other nonverbal, supportive behavior. They should never break in with questions of their own, no matter how interested they may be in the topic under discussion. At this stage of the interview, it does not matter at all what candidates say, so long as they take over the conversation. Should their conversation come to a halt, interviewers can perhaps keep it going a little longer by repeating a part of the original broad question that has so far been unanswered. Small talk ranging from two to three minutes is usually sufficient to ease whatever nervousness a candidate may have initially experienced. The sound of one's own voice in a strange situation usually helps to develop confidence, ease initial tension, and build rapport. When candidates are not immediately put on the spot by being asked to tell about some more serious aspect of their background, they do not feel the need to sell themselves, and, thus, they have the chance to relax and chat informally about matters of no great concern.

COMPREHENSIVE INTRODUCTORY QUESTIONS

The comprehensive introductory question represents the single most important technique for getting candidates to do most of the talking. This type of question is so comprehensive that many candidates can talk several minutes and still not answer all aspects of it.

Once the small talk has come to an end, interviewers bridge the gap between the small talk and the first introductory question with a comment such as "Let me tell you a little bit about our conversation today." They then direct the conversation to the real purpose of the session by making an appropriate opening remark. This should include a statement of the company's interest in placing new employees in positions that make the best use of their ability. It should present an overview of the interview by pointing out that the discussion will include as much relevant information as possible about work history, education, and interests.

Then the interviewer can lead into the question with a statement such as the following: "In this company, we believe that the more information we can obtain about people applying for work, the better able we will be to place them in a position that makes best use of their abilities. I would therefore like to have you tell me everything you can about your work experience, education, training, and present interests."

Having provided the candidate with the purpose of the interview, the interviewer launches into a discussion of previous work experience, the first topic that appears on the Interview Guide (see Appendix). This is accomplished with a comprehensive introductory question; for example, "Suppose you begin by telling me about your previous jobs, starting with the first job and working up to the present. I would be interested in how you obtained each job, your duties and responsibilities, level of earnings, likes and dislikes, and any special achievements along the way." The very comprehensive nature of the question gives candidates the basis for a considerable amount of discussion. As indicated above, it represents the single most important factor in getting them to talk for as much as 85 percent of the interview time.

After the discussion of work experience has been completed, interviewers should launch into the second topic for discussion—education. A question such as the following will do the job here: "Suppose you tell me about your education. I'd be interested in the subjects you liked best, those you didn't, what your grades were, and why you decided (or decided not) to explore postgraduate education." Candidates are not expected to remember every single item in the introductory question.

They will often have to be reminded, for example, to discuss subject preferences or asked to talk at greater length about community service. Such follow-up questions, though, are simply reminders of some of the things candidates have been initially asked to talk about. As such, they do not represent new questions and hence do not require quite so much concentration on the candidate's part.

THE IMPORTANCE OF MEMORIZATION

Interviewers are advised to memorize verbatim the questions presented above. This will make their interviews a lot smoother, and because they do not have to concern themselves with formulating such questions, they are much more free to listen to what candidates have to say.

ASSUME CONSENT

During the introductory questions, interviewers should do everything they can to sell the candidates on the desirability of providing honest information. They should consciously use appropriate facial expressions and tonal intonations. And their very manner should assume consent.

Just as an effective salesperson assumes that the customer wants to buy, so the expert interviewer assumes that candidates will be happy to respond to all of his or her questions. Questions are best phrased positively, in such a way that there is no alternative but to answer them. The phrase "Suppose you tell me" is always more effective than the phrase, "I wonder if you would be willing to tell me." The latter choice of words provides the alternative of not answering and thus fails to assume consent. Also, it gives the impression that the interviewer is not confident and thus may not be certain whether or not he or she should ask the question.

The techniques discussed in this chapter are almost foolproof in terms of getting spontaneous information and getting the candidate to do the major share of the talking. Interviewers who study these techniques carefully and use them as described will often be quite amazed how successful they can be.

THE CALCULATED PAUSE

We have mentioned that interviewers should wait out candidates who stop talking without having answered all parts of a multifaceted question. This is called the *calculated pause* and is used as a conscious technique. Interviewers without much experience tend to become uncomfortable whenever a slight pause in the conversation occurs and are therefore likely to break in prematurely with unnecessary comments or questions. But experienced interviewers purposely permit a pause to occur from time to time, because they know that candidates will frequently elaborate on a previous point rather than allow the discussion to come to a standstill. The candidate often senses that the interviewer's silence calls for a fuller treatment of the topic under consideration.

In the conscious use of the pause, interviewers must not break eye contact. If they look down at their guide, candidates naturally assume that they are formulating another question and, hence, wait for that question to be articulated. However, if interviewers do not break eye contact and look expectant as the pause elongates, candidates feel a certain degree of pressure and usually search quickly for something else to say. Obviously, if candidates fail to respond within a few seconds, interviewers should relieve the pressure by asking another question. To do otherwise might risk a loss of rapport.

Under normal circumstances, the calculated pause is remarkably effective in drawing out spontaneous information. Equally important, interviewers have to do less talking when they use an occasional pause and, therefore, perfect the art of becoming good listeners. Once perfected, the calculated pause is a powerful technique, particularly when not used too frequently. It also has wide application outside the interview situation. It is a useful tool for salespeople in determining a customer's needs, it is widely used in the legal profession, and it is a valuable technique for use in labor negotiations for determining what is on the other person's mind.

FACIAL EXPRESSIONS

Interviewers should look expectant as a means of making the calculated pause effective, but looking expectant and being facially responsive are conscious techniques that should be utilized throughout the interview. Anyone can manage an expectant look by lifting the eyebrows a little and smiling slightly. This expression gives the interviewer the appearance of being receptive and serves as a powerful tool in getting the subject to open up. People who are facially responsive react facially as well as verbally to another individual's comment. When that individual smiles, the interviewer should smile; when the candidate talks about an unfortunate experience, the interviewer's face should show concern.

Facial expressions play a particularly important role when asking questions that border on the personal. The edge is taken off a delicate or personal question when it is posed with a half smile with the eyebrows raised. And, as we shall see later on, facial expressions are of paramount importance in probing for an individual's shortcomings. Finally, facial expressions help to give one the appearance of being understanding, sympathetic, and receptive. There are some individuals, in fact, who are so adroit with facial expressions that they are able to keep the subject talking almost by that means alone. It is a matter of fact that some people's countenances are naturally more animated than others. Thus, some people find it necessary to work at being facially responsive, while others find it very natural.

People being trained as interviewers sometimes raise the question, "Isn't it possible that I will look like a phony if I try too hard to become facially responsive?" The answer to this, of course, is a qualified "yes." Facial expressions, as in the case of all other conscious techniques, can be overdone and can give interviewers the appearance of being artificial and insincere. Experience has shown, however, that most people do not use enough facial expression. It is the rare person indeed who tends to overplay this kind of interviewing technique.

When we stop to realize that there are only two means at our disposal for getting through to people in social situations—facial expressions and voice—it certainly behooves all of us to make maximum utilization of whatever talents we have in these two important areas. One has only to look at television programs to note how effective people can be who have had specific training in vocal and facial expression. Although most of us cannot approach this professional level, we can do a lot more with our faces and with our voices than we are currently doing. Conscious effort along these lines can pay big dividends in improved interpersonal relationships.

VOICE

The art of persuasion relies heavily upon the voice. In the interview, we use every means at our disposal to persuade candidates to reveal all their qualifications and characteristics—shortcomings as well as assets. In their attempts to improve vocal effectiveness, interviewers must keep two things in mind: (1) they must not talk too loudly, and (2) they should try to use all ranges of the voice.

When interviewers talk too loudly, they tend to threaten candidates to some extent and to push them off center stage, relegating them to a minor role. Since interviewers do not want that to happen, they should try to keep their voices at a rather low conversational level, in that way encouraging the candidate to take over, since candidates should do some 85 percent of the talking and should therefore be "front and center" during the entire interview.

It is much easier to teach people to speak more softly than it is to teach them to use all ranges of their voices. In particular, interviewers should concentrate on greater utilization of the upper range of the voice. When candidates are asked questions or given compliments, for example, interviewers should try to use the upper range of the voice. When the voice is consciously placed in the upper register, rather than mumbled or "swallowed," the comment takes on greater significance. It has the effect of making the interviewer sound more impressed with the candidate's achievement. This has the long-range effect of building so much rapport that candidates subsequently become more willing to discuss some of their shortcomings. People do not mind talking about some of their problems if they are absolutely certain that the listener is completely aware of their successes.

As in the case of facial expressions, vocal intonations should mirror the candidate's moods. When candidates discuss unfortunate or unhappy aspects of their background, the interviewer's voice should take on a sympathetic tone, and when candidates divulge something of a highly personal nature, the interviewer's voice should reflect an understanding quality. Complete responsiveness on the part of the interviewer has an unusually powerful effect upon the other person, making that individual not only willing but often actually anxious to talk about things that are uppermost in her or his mind.

Of course, vocal inflection can be overdone, which should be avoided at all costs because it gives the impression of insincerity and may have the effect of alienating individuals rather than attracting them. Again, though, it is the rare person who falls into this trap. Most of us do not use sufficient vocal intonation and hence could profit from training in this area. For many years, General Electric has sponsored a course called "Effective Presentation." This course, which involves the proper use of the voice in business specific situations, has been one of the most popular courses in the GE training program, with some people finding it so helpful that they have taken it a second time. Interviewers would be well advised to take courses of this nature if such courses exist in their organization.

POSITIVE REINFORCEMENT

There is perhaps no more powerful tool in the interviewer's arsenal than commenting positively on a candidate's achievements. Some people in the field refer to this as "stroking," some call it "reinforcement," and others just refer to it as "giving the candidate a pat on the back."

Reinforcement can be both verbal and nonverbal. Comments such as "Very impressive!" or "You deserve a lot of credit for that!" or "Excellent!" give candidates the feeling that their achievements are being appropriately recognized, and they respond accordingly. Such achievements as high grades, job promotions, unusually long hours spent on a given job, or election to an honorary society should be recognized by the interviewer. When achievements are recognized by interviewers in the form of a compliment, candidates often visibly warm to the discussion and become increasingly expansive and spontaneous. To be appreciated is a human need, and the job candidate is no exception in this respect.

Responses that reinforce can also be *nonverbal*. Frequent head nodding and sounds of affirmation such as "Uh-huh" and "Hmmm" help candidates feel that interviewers are paying attention and appreciate what they are saying. Actually, one-word interjections such as "Fine!" "Terrific!" or "Impressive!" can be worked into the discussion without interrupting the candidate at all. The frequency with which forms of reinforcement are utilized during the interview depends largely on the candidate's makeup. If the person were a relatively sophisticated, secure individual, a considerable amount of reinforcement would not be appropriate or needed. In such a case, nonverbal reinforcement and a few verbalized comments would normally be sufficient. If a candidate were insecure and relatively unsophisticated, a great deal more reinforcement would be in order. However, because of this candidate's deficiencies, he or she might not be the best one for the job anyway.

Chapter Six | Probing More Deeply for Behavioral Clues

Comprehensive introductory questions are designed to launch the discussion in each area of the interview, but those questions, of course, will by no means do the entire job. Interviewers must use *follow-up questions*—questions that follow the comprehensive introductory question—to keep candidates talking and to probe more deeply for clues to behavior. Follow-up questions are used to prod candidates from time to time, helping them reveal their life story to the fullest extent and become more definitive concerning its important aspects.

Interviewers' remarks should be interjected so artfully that they seldom, if ever, assume center stage. Rather, they dart in and out with such facility that candidates seldom become aware of the fact that their conversation is being directed.

INTERVIEWING AS CONVERSATION

Interviewing is conversation between two people. It is not an interrogation. Whenever a comment can be substituted for a question, in fact, conversation flows more smoothly and interviewers lessen the impression of being investigative in their approach. Interviewers are just that, interviewers, not private detectives. If they want more information on a given subject, they can frequently get such information by the simple comment, "That sounds very interesting." So encouraged, candidates are quite likely to provide further elaboration without having been specifically asked to do so. There is certainly nothing wrong with asking questions, but comments, interspersed with questions, provide more variety and help the interview seem more natural.

KEEP QUESTIONS AND COMMENTS OPEN-ENDED

A leading question such as "Did you rank pretty high in your high school class?" makes it difficult for the candidate to give a negative response. Since the interviewer has asked a leading question, the candidate is greatly tempted to say, "Yes." The candidate whose grades were poor, and who honestly admits it, may realize at once that this could create a negative impression and may become uncomfortable in the interview situation and unwilling to offer any more potentially negative information.

In order to avoid such leading comments or questions, the interviewer should keep remarks open-ended. Remember: an open-ended question is one that does not telegraph an anticipated response and that leaves the candidate free to discuss either favorable or unfavorable information.

There is a wonderful phrase—"To what extent"—that makes any question open-ended. Instead of using a leading question such as "Were you successful on that job?" the question can be made open-ended by saying, "To what extent were you successful on that job?" Or, instead of saying, "Did you enjoy that experience?" one might say, "To what extent did you find that experience satisfying?"

There is another remarkably effective way to ensure an open-ended response—the use of the question: "How did you *feel about* that situation?" When you say, "Did you like the people there?" you push the person to say, "Yes." But, when you say, "How did you feel about the people there?" you can anticipate an objective response.

TALK THE APPLICANT'S LANGUAGE

There is no quicker way to lose rapport than to use words that are outside the applicant's vocabulary. The applicant becomes quickly confused and is made to feel inferior. Interviewers who are good listeners can determine an applicant's range of vocabulary in a relatively short period of time and subsequently make every effort to use words the applicant readily understands.

QUESTIONS AND COMMENTS MUST BE WORK-RELATED

To stay within EEOC guidelines, questions must be primarily concerned with the relevance of an applicant's work history and education to the job under consideration. The primary concern should be the extent to which applicants can handle a job and will make mature, stable employees. Questions should not be asked about specific age, marital status, number of dependents, or personal finances.

A work-related question, on the other hand, would be one whose purpose is to determine how well applicants have performed on their previous jobs or in school. This kind of question provides strong clues about an individual's ability to handle a job for which he or she is being considered, and so is obviously work-related and therefore perfectly legal.

FUNCTION OF FOLLOW-UP QUESTIONS

As we have already seen, the function of follow-up remarks is essentially to help applicants present a clear picture of their qualifications. By means of adroit questioning, interviewers must be able to draw out applicants so that they can present their real assets. Equally important, interviewers must be able to structure the discussion so that they get a clear picture of candidates' shortcomings. Within this broad framework of objectives, however, follow-up remarks serve a number of specific functions.

Reminding the Candidate of Omitted Parts of Comprehensive Introductory Questions

The questions that are used to introduce the discussion in each of the major interviewing areas are so comprehensive that candidates will often forget to discuss some of the items in response to the comprehensive introductory question alone. Usually they will have to be reminded to discuss such job factors as likes, dislikes, earnings, and accomplishments. And they may have to be reminded to discuss such things as subject preferences, grades, and extracurricular activities.

Then, there are other items listed under each interviewing area on the Interview Guide that may have to be brought to the candidate's attention in follow-up questions. For example, if a candidate fails to tell why he or she left a certain job, the interviewer will have to bring this up in the form of a casual follow-up question.

Getting Further Work and Education Information Relevant to the Job

We have already noted that the interviewer must have a clear mental picture of the job description and behavior specifications at the time a candidate's qualifications for a given job are discussed. As the interview progresses, the extent to which the candidate's work history and education match up to the job "specs" at hand should be noted. The candidate will not know which aspects of his or her background to emphasize, in terms of establishing the relevance of past performance to future work responsibilities, since he or she has not been acquainted with these specifications. The interviewer must therefore be helpful in this regard.

To use an example, let us assume that technically trained people are being interviewed for a job that involves a considerable amount of report writing. In this case, the interviewer would use follow-up questions in an effort to determine the amount of report writing a given candidate has done in previous jobs and the degree of writing facility acquired. The interviewer would, of course, try to mask the intent of the questions with appropriate phrasing and casual, offhand presentation. It could be phrased, "In connection with your research and development work with that company, was there more emphasis placed on the actual technical experimentation or on the writing of results?"

After the discussion the interviewer might add, "How did you feel about your accomplishments there? Did you feel you were relatively more effective in the actual experimentation or in the report writing?" Even though the candidate may feel that he or she made the greatest contribution in laboratory experimental work, information concerning report-writing ability will usually be volunteered in response to such a question. And he or she will often place a relatively objective value judgment on writing ability, particularly since it will not be clear how important this may be for the job in question.

Clarifying the True Meaning of a Candidate's Casual Remarks

Clues to the candidate's behavior will not always be clear-cut. In response to a question concerning job dislikes, for example, a candidate may say that detail work was less satisfying. However, the interviewer cannot assume from such a remark that the candidate cannot do detail work. The interviewer must try to pin down this clue by fixing the *degree* of dislike.

In this case, a response to the original remark could be "Many people find detail work much less interesting than other aspects of their job." This kind of sympathetic response often encourages the candidate to elaborate. In so doing, an intense dislike of detail may be revealed in the form of an open acknowledgment that he or she is not very proficient in the type of work that requires close attention to detail. Or the candidate may indicate that, while not enjoying detail, he or she nevertheless finds it relatively easy to carry out when it is an important part of the job. The interpretation of these two responses would be quite different. The first response, if supported by other clues pointing in the same direction, would lead the interviewer to the possible conclusion that the candidate was not a good detail person. The second response would lead to no such conclusion.

Searching for Support of Early Established Hypotheses

Highly skilled interviewers often pick up little clues to the candidate's possible behavior relatively early in the discussion, and these clues help them establish a hypothesis with respect to the possible existence of certain assets or liabilities. They know, however, that such hypotheses must be supported by more tangible evidence. Interviewers therefore use exploratory questions to probe for clues that might support their hypothesis. If none is found, they must, of course, discard that hypothesis and search for new ones.

For purposes of illustration, we will assume that the interviewer has obtained some initial impressions of the candidate that point in the direction of superficiality, lack of depth, and limited powers of analysis. As he leads the candidate from area to area, he will, of course, be on the lookout for supporting evidence or for the lack of it. From time to time, he will interject so-called "depth questions"—questions that require a fair amount of analysis. For example, he may ask the candidate what a job has to have in order to give the candidate satisfaction. Or he may ask what gains in terms of personality development accrued as a result of military experience. If the candidate's responses to a series of such questions reveal little ability to dig beneath the surface, the interviewer may rightly conclude that the individual is indeed superficial and without much ability to analyze.

Suppose that an interviewer has formed an early hypothesis that a candidate may be somewhat lazy. Let us say that she has arrived at this tentative judgment because of the man's professed unwillingness to work long hours. In order to check and support this initial hypothesis, the interviewer will use follow-up questions to probe specifically for such factors as (1) how much effort the candidate may have expended on other jobs, (2) how hard he studied in school, and (3) any demonstrated willingness to carry out constructive tasks either at home or in the community after putting in a regular work day.

If she finds that the candidate (1) took the easy way out to avoid tackling difficult problems, (2) studied just hard enough to get by, or (3) decided against graduate work because it would have meant going to school at night—if she is able to get consistent information of this kind—she is able to document her views concerning the candidate's lack of motivation. The point to remember here, though, is that this kind of information probably would not have been brought to light had it not been for the fact that the interviewer probed for the appropriate clues by means of follow-up questions.

Quantifying Information

In the effort to document the findings with respect to the candidate's behavior, it is important to get definitive responses. When successes, failures, or even reactions are spoken about in general terms, therefore, the interviewer must get more specific answers. For example, if the candidate simply indicates that his grades in college were "above average," a good follow-up question would be: "Does that mean that your grades ranked you in the top 10 percent of your class, the upper quarter, the upper third, or perhaps the upper half?" Or, if a candidate merely indicates that she was given a raise in salary after her first six months on the job, the interviewer must follow through with "What did that amount to in terms of dollars?" Again, if a candidate indicates being "out of work for a while," it is important to establish how long the unemployment actually lasted. Wherever possible, try to get numbers: for example, the number of hours worked on a part-time job while attending school, specific test scores, class standing, or number of students in the graduating class.

KINDS OF PROBING QUESTIONS

We mentioned previously that many interviewers fail to probe beneath the surface because they do not have the tools to do the job. The material that follows provides such tools in the form of three kinds of extremely important questions.

1. The Laundry-List Question

Candidates almost invariably find some areas more difficult to discuss than others. Confronted with a question that requires considerable analysis, they frequently "block" and find it somewhat difficult to come up with an immediate response. In such a situation, the interviewer comes to the candidate's assistance with a *laundry-list* question. As the name implies, this kind of question suggests a variety of possible responses and permits subjects to choose among them.

For example, if the candidate blocks on the question, "What are some of the things that a job has to have to give you satisfaction?" the interviewer may stimulate thinking by such a laundry-list comment as "Well, you know, some people are more interested in money, some want security, others enjoy working as a member of a team, and others like a job that takes them out of doors a good bit of the time. What's important to you?" Given a variety of possible responses, candidates are normally able to get their thoughts together and supply a considerable amount of information.

The laundry-list question can also be used as a means of confirming clues to behavior that the interviewer has obtained from some previous aspects of the discussion. Let us assume, for example, that a candidate has dropped some hints that seem to indicate a dislike for detail. The interviewer can often follow up on such clues by including a reference to detail in the laundry-list question at the end of the discussion of work history.

For example, the interviewer may say, "What are some of the things that a job has to have in order to give you satisfaction? Some people want to manage, whereas others are more interested in an opportunity to come up with new ideas; some like to work regular hours, whereas others do not mind spending additional hours on a job even though that might interfere with family life; some like to work with details while others do not; some are quite happy working at a desk while others prefer to move around a good bit—what's important to you?"

If, in response to the above question, the candidate said, "Well, I do not want anything that involves a lot of detail; actually, I'm not at all good at that type of work," the interviewer would certainly have obtained further confirmation of the subject's reaction to detail. The very fact that the individual selected this item for discussion reflects the importance she attaches to it. If the candidate were being considered for a job where attention to detail figured importantly in the specifications, her response would reveal a serious shortcoming for that job.

Besides taking a candidate off the hook by alleviating the tendency to block, the laundry-list question also has the further function of spelling out to the candidate what the interviewer specifically has in mind. By the very nature of the items used in the series of possible responses, the interviewer encourages the candidate to respond specifically rather than generally and makes certain that the responses will be helpful in the evaluation of the individual.

Toward the end of the candidate's discussion of work history, for example, the interviewer may ask him what he has learned about his strengths as a result of working on various jobs. In order to tell the candidate what the interviewer specifically has in mind, he uses such a laundry list as "Did you find that you worked a little harder than the average individual, got along better with people, organized things better, gave better attention to detail—just what?" Such a laundry-list question helps to tie down individuals' responses, so that they talk in terms of traits of personality, motivation, or character.

2. Two-Step Probing for the "Why"

The "why" question represents our best tool for developing evidence of analytical and critical thinking. With the first step, we proceed from the general to the specific. Experienced interviewers know that *why* an individual took some course of action is frequently more revealing than *what* he or she did, because the reasons people do things tell us a great deal about their judgment, their motivation, and other factors of their personality structure. Probing for why a candidate left a given job, for example, may provide clues to such factors as inability to relate to authority (problems with the boss), inability to do the work, dissatisfaction with close supervision, or the kind of restlessness that motivates a person to move on to something new.

When, for example, candidates leave a job before obtaining another one, a "why" question may reveal a tendency to rationalize, to try to explain away one's failure. A reply such as "I couldn't very well look for a new job while working eight hours a day on the present job," taken even at face value, indicates poor judgment and immaturity. But it also may be a cover for precipitative action based on a quick temper or even for having been fired.

It is not only important to find out what candidates liked or disliked about their jobs, but perhaps more important still to learn the why of their likes or dislikes. This is what is meant by probing more deeply.

If a woman indicates that she liked working with computers, for example, a good why question would be "What is there about working with computers that appeals to you?" Such a question may reveal that she has a flair for mathematics, that she enjoys problem solving, that she appreciates the accuracy and thoroughness that are a part of such detailed work, or that she enjoys an opportunity to work on her own without close supervision.

When a man indicates a dislike of mathematics in school, a question such as "What was there about math that turned you off?" would be in order. A reply such as "I never could understand what I was supposed to do" could conceivably provide a clue to mental ability.

When a candidate indicates that she has an ability to get along with people, the interviewer should dig deeper by saying, "What traits do you have that make it possible for you to get along with people as well as you do?" The reply to that question may reveal such valuable traits as tact, empathy, or sensitivity to the needs of others.

"Why" questions should be used sparingly throughout the interview, though. Rarely is there sufficient time to probe for the why of everything the candidate says. In addition, frequent use of this technique puts too much pressure on the candidate and results in the feeling that he or she is being grilled. The technique must be reserved for probing in the most fruitful areas. These areas obviously differ from person to person, but with practice and experience, interviewers will learn how to recognize fruitful areas for further probing when they occur.

3. Double-Edged Questions

Having asked candidates to reveal their strengths, one can logically follow up with a question about shortcomings, which can be presented as a laundry-list question, with the double-edged question used as a follow-up. Thus, an interviewer might say, "What are some of the things about yourself that you would like to improve? Would you like to develop more self-confidence, acquire more tact, learn to control your temper better, improve your attendance record—just what?" If the candidate finds it difficult to answer this question, the interviewer may probe more specifically with a double-edged question such as, "What about tact? Do you have as much of that as you would like to have, or is this something you could improve a little bit?" Given something specific to talk about, most candidates tend to respond quite spontaneously and often reveal a good bit about their shortcomings.

Double-edged questioning is used to make it easy for candidates to admit their shortcomings and to help them achieve greater self-insight. The questions are double-edged in the sense that they make it possible for the subject to choose between two possible responses. Moreover, the positive alternative is usually phrased in such a way that the subject would not choose that alternative without feeling they had the ability or personality trait in question to a fairly high degree. The more negative alternative is phrased so that it is easy for the candidate to choose that alternative, even though it is the more undesirable of the two possible responses.

In interviewing people for lower-level office jobs, interviewers often find quite revealing a double-edged question such as "What about your ability to spell? Do you have that ability to the extent that you would like, or is that something you could improve a little bit?" How confident the individual may be in her or his ability to spell is often revealed in tone of voice or facial expressions. If there is any hesitancy in the reply or if the person frowns, this may be indicative of a problem area. The point here, though, is that the double-edged question was used to launch this discussion. Most people find it much easier to discuss things that they could improve rather than qualities that they lack. Thus phrased, the double-edged question represents an adroit way to introduce the subject of shortcomings.

HOW TO SOFTEN DIRECT QUESTIONS

Some interviewers tend to be too blunt and direct in their questioning.

Since this risks a possible loss of rapport, such questions can be soft-ened by the use of appropriate *introductory phrases* and *qualifying words*. Such introductory phrases as the following will help to soften almost any direct question:

    Is it possible that...?

    How did you happen to...?

    Has there been any opportunity to...?

    To what do you attribute...?

Qualifying words and phrases such as "might," "perhaps," "to some extent," "somewhat," and "a little bit" are also effective in soft-ening direct questions.

A study of the two types of questions listed below will show how the direct question has been softened by means of introductory phrases and qualifying words. The questions on the left are too direct; those on the right are more appropriate.

Too Direct	**More Appropriate**
1. Why did you leave that job?	1. *How did you happen* to leave that job?
2. Why do you think you had trouble with your boss?	2. *To what do you attribute* the minor difficulties you exper-ienced with your supervisor?
3. How much time did you save your employer by doing things differently?	3. To what extent were there opportunities to save your employer time by doing things differently?
4. Why did you decide to take a cut in pay in order to get transferred to that other job?	4. *What prompted your decision* to take a cut in pay in order to get transferred to that other job?
5. Do you lack self-confidence?	5. To what extent is self-confi-dence a trait that you might want to improve?
6. Are you overly sensitive?	6. How might you be overly sensitive to criticism?

Note-Taking

Discussion of the techniques of the interview would not be complete without some reference to the taking of notes. This subject, incidentally, has stirred a considerable amount of controversy over the years, some authorities claiming that note-taking results in a loss of rapport and others indicating that the interviewer should feel free to take as many notes as he or she desires.

We take the view that there is no reason at all why trained interviewers should not be able to take as many notes as they deem necessary. One who has achieved genuine skill in the use of such techniques as facial and vocal expression, pats on the back, playing down of unfavorable information, and appropriate questioning should be able to take notes in such a way that candidates become almost unaware of this activity, usually becoming so absorbed in the discussion that they take little notice of the skilled interviewer's note-taking.

However, any writing done by interviewers should be carried out as unobtrusively as possible. They should keep pad and pencil in clear view at all times, while minimizing extraneous hand movements. The simple movement of placing the pencil on the desk and picking it up at frequent intervals can often be distracting. In terms of content, notes should be made only when candidates relate objective data concerning their background or when they tell about their past achievements. Whenever they impart information of a highly personal or derogatory nature, interviewers should obviously refrain from any writing. Rather, interviewers should wait until candidates volunteer the next bit of favorable information and, at that time, record both the favorable information and the unfavorable data previously obtained. Skilled interviewers learn to record their findings without breaking eye contact for more than a few seconds at a time. This places the note-taking function in its proper perspective, as a seemingly minor aspect of the interview.

EEOC Considerations

1. Keep questions job-related.
2. Do not ask questions of minorities or females that you would not ask of nonminorities or males.

---

3. Never ask questions out of curiosity alone. All questions should have a valid purpose.
4. Never ask a single female about her plans for marriage.
5. Never ask a female if she has someone to care for her children while she works or what her plans are for having children.
6. Do not ask an older worker how many more years he or she plans to work. This could be construed as age discrimination.
7. If the job involves travel, working long hours, or potential transfer, attitudes toward such conditions cannot be asked of females alone. If this question is to be used, it must be used with all applicants—males and females alike.

Probing is at the heart of the interview process. However, it is still important to realize that not all questions are appropriate to ask. In Chapter 9 we will be discussing questions you cannot ask in an interview.

Chapter Seven | Techniques of Control

I n the two previous chapters devoted to the techniques of the interview, emphasis has been placed primarily on ways and means of getting the applicant to talk freely. This, of course, represents a first objective. The interviewer can learn little unless the applicant talks spontaneously.

Spontaneous discourse in itself, however, is not sufficient. Discussion must be guided and channeled in such a way that applicants tell what the interviewer needs to learn rather than simply what they themselves want to relate. Indeed, it is quite possible for an applicant to talk as long as three hours in an uncontrolled situation without giving as much salient and evaluative information as could have been provided in one and a half hours of guided conversation.

Teaching interviewers how to exercise optimum control during the evaluation interview represents one of the most difficult tasks in the entire training procedure. During the early stages of their training, interviewers invariably exercise too little control. In their desire to get spontaneous information, they are inclined to let candidates go on and on, just as long as they talk freely. As a consequence, the interview suffers from lack of intensive coverage in the important areas and from lack of balance. There is too much emphasis on one area of the applicant's background and too little on others. In addition, such an interview takes far too much time.

With proper training, interviewers gradually learn to use just the right amount of guidance and control, tactfully and unobtrusively. In the very early stages of the interview, they permit candidates to talk quite freely, even though some of the resulting information may not be particularly relevant. They do this in order to set the pattern of letting candidates do most of the talking. Once this pattern has been established, though, they do not hesitate to interject comments and questions at critical points, in order to ensure intensive coverage and sufficient penetration in each area of the candidate's background.

Thus, measures of control are designed to (1) ensure adequate coverage of each area of the candidate's background, (2) secure appropriate penetration into the truly salient aspects of the candidate's previous experiences, and (3) utilize the interviewer's time efficiently and economically.

APPROPRIATE COVERAGE

Some candidates build up such a head of steam that they tend to take over the interview and run away with it. In so doing, they may skip over some important areas too quickly and leave out other factors entirely, discussing only what they want to tell rather than what the interviewer needs to know. When candidates begin to take charge and to race over their history too rapidly, the interviewer should step in and control the situation, tactfully reminding such a person to discuss likes and dislikes on each job, reason for leaving, and so on. Otherwise the individual could conceivably cover an entire area such as work experience in as few as 10 minutes, without providing any real clues to behavior or any substantial information about accumulated skills.

BALANCE

During the early stages of their training, interviewers frequently fail to apportion interviewing time appropriately. They permit the candidates to spend far too much time on one area of their background and far too little on some of the other areas. Such interviews lack balance. In an insufficiently controlled interview, some candidates find it quite easy to spend as much as one and a half hours discussing their previous jobs. In so doing, they naturally include a lot of unnecessary and irrelevant information. When this occurs, the interviewer suddenly realizes that too much time has been spent on the work area. Then, in order to complete the discussion within a reasonable period of time, they push the candidate through the other background areas too rapidly. The ensuing lack of interview balance precludes comprehensive evaluation of the individual's overall qualifications.

It is not reasonable to expect all information supplied by applicants to be relevant. Of necessity, much of the discussion provides little more than a framework to be used as a basis for probing into more fruitful areas. At the same time, interviewers must continually guard against excessive and irrelevant detail. They must continually ask themselves, "Am I learning anything about the candidate's behavior or anything about the extent to which he or she meets the job specifications, as a result of this particular segment of the discussion?" If the answer is "No," the candidate must tactfully be pushed along to another topic.

In order to achieve proper balance, interviewers should place a clock on the table, and they should casually refer to it at frequent intervals. Time spent in the various interview areas with candidates for higher-level jobs should be apportioned roughly as indicated below. (These time limits can be appreciably shortened in interviews with candidates for lower-level positions—usually 40 to 45 minutes.)

Work history—55 to 65 minutes
Education—15 to 20 minutes
Present social adjustment—5 to 10 minutes

The above timetable permits a minimum of one hour and 15 minutes and a maximum of one hour and 35 minutes. It must be emphasized, though, that these time allowances are to be used only as a rough guide. Since there are marked differences between individuals, it will obviously take longer to interview one person than another.

Factors that influence interviewing time requirements are primarily those of age and psychological complexity of the individual. Older applicants normally require more time because they have more experiences to be discussed and evaluated. Regardless of age, the individual who is complex psychologically requires greater time because there are more facets of the personality to be considered.

There are cases, too, where the suggested timetable may have to be modified with respect to the amount of time required for a given interview area. If the candidate is fresh out of college, for example, and has had few summer or other part-time jobs, it will obviously be unnecessary to spend as much as 55 minutes on the work history area. In evaluating such an individual, proportionately more time should be spent on education and on the other areas of the background.

DESCRIPTIVE VS. EVALUATIVE INFORMATION

In general, candidates supply two types of information—descriptive and evaluative. If the interview is not sufficiently controlled, almost all the information may be of a descriptive nature. Candidates may describe the companies for which they have previously worked, go into elaborate details concerning job duties, and talk a lot about the fun they had in college. Some of this descriptive information serves a purpose, but it does not tell us much about the individual's makeup.

Interviewers must control the discussion to get evaluative information, which can be used as a basis for determining the candidate's personality, character, and motivation. By artful and tactful questioning, they must penetrate to the candidate's basic reactions to key situations, with a view to determining the possible effects of those situations on the individual's growth and development. The interviewer must find a way to cut off descriptive information and probe more deeply for evaluative data.

CONTROLLING THE TIME

Good interviewers are always jealous of their time. Although they must not in any way convey this fact to the applicant, they nevertheless use control in order to complete interviews in the shortest possible time and still get the best possible picture of the candidate's qualifications. For example, the interview that runs for two and a half to three hours is ordinarily an inefficient one. Such an interview not only consumes more time than is necessary, but results in so much irrelevant detail that interpretation becomes more difficult. In other words, the interviewer has difficulty separating the wheat from the chaff primarily because there is so much chaff.

If interviewers are to assume a normal case load of two to three comprehensive interviews per day, they cannot afford to spend much more than one and a half hours per interview and still have time to write their reports. Moreover, interviewing is a very fatiguing experience because of the attention factor. If interviewers spend too much time on one interview, they will not have sufficient energy to give other candidates the attention they deserve.

The indicated caseload of two to three evaluation interviews per day may strike some as a surprisingly low number. It is true, of course, that employment interviewers can conduct a relatively large number of *preliminary* interviews in a single day. And they can carry out as many as six or seven final interviews on candidates for lower-level plant or office assignments. But it is unreasonable to expect them to do more than three comprehensive interviews per day in the case of persons being considered for higher-level positions. Since the evaluating of key candidates represents such a critical function, it is much better to hire and train additional interviewers than to overload the interviewing staff.

TECHNIQUES OF CONTROL

It is one thing to talk about the need for control and quite another to discuss how it can be accomplished. Fortunately, though, we have two effective techniques to draw upon for this purpose: (1) interruption, and (2) the Interview Guide.

Interruption

When a candidate begins to talk too much—particularly in terms of irrelevant detail and descriptive information—the interview must be controlled by means of interruption. Interruption represents a very effective means of control, but this technique must be employed so subtly that candidates do not realize they are being interrupted. In order to accomplish this, two additional techniques are utilized: timing and positive reinforcement. It is, of course, impolite to interrupt people in the middle of a sentence, and yet if we wait until the end of a sentence, they will already have launched into the next one by the time we get around to interrupting them.

Hence, the interruption must be timed to occur before they have actually completed the sentence. Interviewers therefore learn to interrupt as soon as candidates have completed a thought but before they have a chance to complete the sentence. Moreover, an interruption is always accompanied by a reinforcing comment such as "That's very interesting" or "That must have been very satisfying."

The reinforcing comment represents the introduction to the question that will redirect the discussion and move candidates along to another topic. If, for example, a candidate tells too much about his or her likes on a given job, the interviewer may say, "You must have found that very satisfying. Tell me about some of the things you did not like quite so well."

Thus, timing means anticipating the end of a thought, and reinforcement in this sense means making a positive or favorable comment. Utilization of these two techniques tends to soften the interruption in such a way that candidates may not even realize that they are being interrupted. Because interviewers have commented favorably on a given topic under discussion, candidates are willing to relinquish that topic and permit themselves to be redirected to a new subject. Interviewers should not be too hasty in interrupting applicants when they wander off the track or go into a bit too much detail, because hasty interruption risks the loss of rapport. Give individuals a minute or two to get the uninteresting or irrelevant topic "off their chests" before shutting them off and redirecting their conversation.

Let us assume that a candidate, for example, races lightly over his first two or three jobs, apparently thinking that they are not germane to the discussion. Since this would normally occur at the very beginning of the interview, and since a pattern should be established of having a candidate carry the conversational ball, he would be allowed to talk for three or four minutes. Then, just as he was about to put a period at the end of a sentence, the interviewer would inject a positive comment and redirect him to a more thorough treatment of his first job. The interviewer might say, "You have certainly had some interesting early experiences—so interesting in fact that I would like to know more about them. Suppose you tell me more about your likes, dislikes, and earnings on that first job."

Let us take another example, in which an applicant conceivably wanders off the track and launches prematurely into another interview area. In response to the question, "What did you like best on that job?" she might reply, "I enjoyed the calculations. You know, I am very good in math. I won the math prize in high school and did exceptionally well in calculus. Our high school had two very fine math teachers, and I learned a lot in their classes."

If this woman was not interrupted, she might very easily go on to further discussion of her high school experience and forget all about the discussion of her various jobs. After she has been given a minute or two to discuss her mathematical proficiencies, therefore, the interviewer interrupts by anticipating the end of one of her thoughts with a comment such as "I think it's great that you have such an interest and aptitude in math—particularly since you want to become a systems analyst. Tell me about some of the other things you liked on that job with Carter Steel." Because this candidate has not been interrupted in the middle of a thought, and because she has received a favorable comment about her mathematical proficiency, she would normally be quite willing to be redirected back to her work experience.

Interview Guide

Many inexperienced interviewers approach the interview with no plan at all. They simply pick out some item of the application and go on from there. Such interviews usually suffer from inefficiency and ineffectiveness. Candidates tend to ramble in their discussion and fail to cover some of the more important aspects of their backgrounds.

The Interview Guide, found in the Appendix of this book, provides a "track to run on" and hence represents a very important aspect of control. This guide can bring order, a system, and intensive coverage to a discussion that might otherwise have been inconclusive. The Interview Guide not only specifies the sequence of the discussion, but also includes important factors to be taken up in each major area. The guide is so important that interviewers are advised to keep this form on their laps and refer to it every two or three minutes throughout the interview. This permits the interviewer to use questions on the form verbatim and ensures against omission of important items.

Some interviewers also feel self-conscious about reading questions off the form and try to paraphrase these questions, using their own words. This is a mistake in two respects. First, experience has shown that reading questions from the Interview Guide does not disturb candidates in the least. Second, most interviewers find it very difficult to formulate questions on the spur of the moment that are as effective as the questions in the guide.

GENERAL RULES FOR CONTROL

Candidates obviously vary widely with respect to their interview behavior. It is therefore impossible to discuss all situations where control may be necessary, but there are some general rules that may be applied in almost every case.

Develop a Firm Interviewing Manner

Despite the fact that interviewers only do about 15 percent of the talking, they nevertheless guide the discussion by their very manner and by the way they carry out their role. Although they are friendly, disarming, and permissive, there is a point beyond which they cannot be pushed. By means of vocal and facial expressions, they assume consent. This means that they ask their questions and make their comments in such a way that the applicant is expected to answer. This inner firmness creates an atmosphere of "remote control." That is, interviewers take active control only when they have to, but they are always ready to step in when the occasion demands. Since interviewers are already in the power position—it is the applicant who is seeking the job—they can usually maintain control in a very unobtrusive fashion.

Upon occasion, one meets an applicant who is inclined to be facetious. Such a person may make light of some of the interviewer's questions or may even challenge their relevancy. Such a situation obviously requires firmer control. When a question is challenged or treated facetiously, interviewers should simply restate the question, giving their reasons for asking it. By their general manner rather than by anything they say, interviewers underscore their seriousness of purpose. This approach almost invariably prevails, the applicant becoming very cooperative thereafter. Some applicants like to test the interviewer, just to see how far they can go. Once they determine the point beyond which they cannot go, they usually become very cooperative.

Develop Information Chronologically and Systematically

Candidates, of course, are given considerable freedom in their choice of subject matter, but they should nevertheless be encouraged to supply information chronologically and systematically. In discussing their work experience, for example, they should be asked to start with the very first job and work up to their most recent experience. This not only gives a sense of order to this segment of the interview, but also makes it easier for the interviewer to ascertain the applicant's vocational achievements over the years. In the educational area, it is always best to start with the first years of high school and go on to the subsequent years or even to college if that level of education has been attained. This gives interviewers an opportunity to see how applicants fare as they progress to more difficult academic subject matter and have to compete with more able individuals. The interview guide, of course, spells out the indicated chronology.

Exhaust Each Interview Area Before Going on to the Next One

Constant reference to the Interview Guide helps interviewers get all important information in one area before going on to the next. One might find, for example, after completing the work history, that he or she has neglected to determine an applicant's earnings. The interviewer should go back and get this information before launching into education. When an applicant is permitted to crisscross between areas, it becomes very difficult for interviewers to evaluate total achievement in one area. Moreover, after the applicant has left the room, they invariably find they have forgotten to get some important bit of information.

When omissions do occur and when interviewers do not become aware of this until they are midway into the next area, they should complete the discussion in the current area before going back to get the desired information. To interrupt in the middle of a discussion of education in order to get job earnings breaks the applicant's train of thought and makes it more difficult later for him or her to resume the discussion of education at the point at which it was interrupted.

With Recent College Graduates, Explore Summer Jobs Thoroughly

Many young applicants tend to skip over summer jobs too quickly, feeling they are not relevant to the job for which they are applying, Summer jobs may not be entirely relevant, but they do tell us a great deal about applicants—the initiative they may have demonstrated in getting these jobs, the capacity to adapt to and stay with boring or routine assignments, and the ability to get along with people from diverse backgrounds. Hence, when applicants tend to race over summer experiences, interviewers must use control with a comment such as "I would like to know a lot more about that first summer job—how you got it, what you did, your likes, dislikes, and so forth."

EFFECTIVE CONTROL REQUIRES JUDICIOUS PACING

Here we return to a subject discussed at the beginning of this chapter. If spontaneity of response is to be maintained, control must be exercised tactfully, unobtrusively, and at appropriate intervals. This means that the interviewer must never ask a series of questions one after the other. This gives the appearance of grilling applicants and puts them on the spot. Thus, after asking a penetrating question, the interviewer must find other ways to encourage discussion before asking a second penetrating question. These other ways consist of facial expressions, verbal pats on the back, vocal intonations, and consciously designed pauses.

Although interviewers encourage applicants to talk spontaneously, every once in a while they stop them to keep them on the track or to probe more deeply for salient information. Then they immediately give them their head, encouraging them to carry on. In short, they consciously pace the interview in such a way that they get all the necessary information without pressing the applicant and without losing rapport.

SPECIAL CONSIDERATIONS

If you have difficulty establishing rapport with a candidate, perhaps because you feel you have little in common with her or him, do not control quite as strictly. Permit such candidates to talk freely, even if the discourse tends to ramble and be descriptive in nature. Although this will result in more "chaff" along with the "wheat" and will take more time, it will nevertheless provide more clues to behavior than would have come to light in an interview that was more strictly controlled.

With applicants who are particularly sensitive about the possibility that they may not be hired, interviewers should be especially adroit in the manner in which they interrupt such applicants for purposes of control. The timing and positive reinforcement that are a part of interruption must be handled with great care. A sensitive person who feels he or she has been cut off may interpret the cause of the interruption as a function of race, sex, or a disability rather than as a function of completing the interview on time.

Chapter Eight | Behavioral Interviewing Techniques

The term "behavioral interviewing" has been around for over 30 years, so this approach and concept are not new. It was coined at a time when interviewing was taking on heightened importance in the selection process. With the lowest unemployment since the 1970s, even the best companies were struggling to fill all of their positions. The process was used to identify specific behaviors that would either be a strength or weakness for a specific position and help to zero in on a candidate's ability to do the job. It was used then, and is being used today, to minimize bias by maximizing facts. This helps to increase the potential of matching a person's skills to the requirements of the job.

The behavioral interviewing questions are used to get at a truer understanding of who the candidate really is. The technique uses specific examples and accomplishments from the candidate's work history.

Today, there are hundreds of organizations, from outplacement firms to résumé and career firms, who help people develop résumés. This level of professionalism may make it difficult for interviewers to truly understand the quality of the individual in the preselection process. What role did the candidate play in achieving the accomplishment? Was it done alone or with others? What behaviors were being demonstrated, from leadership to results orientation to planning and organization? Using behavior-based questions enables the interviewer to get data to evaluate and assess, and to make objective comparisons between candidates.

THE CANDIDATE AND THE BEHAVIORAL INTERVIEW

For a candidate, behavioral interviewing requires an understanding of one's accomplishments and how they were achieved. Too often job applicants are very superficial in identifying their skills and competencies and can come across as quite weak. To be successful here, applicants need to demonstrate what they did, how they did it, and the results that were achieved.

Reviewing specific past behavior on the job is especially important given the fact that many candidates have been trained in interviewing and are likely to give "socially desirable" answers they think you want to hear, as contrasted to what they actually did on the job and the influence or impact they had. Many candidates may look good on paper with respect to their work experience, training, and education, but have little substance when asked how they fulfilled their roles and the processes they used.

STUDYING THE JOB

The first and critical step in doing behavioral interviewing is to study the job to be filled. To predict job performance, we must know the job requirements and the characteristics that are relevant to the job. What tasks or results are we looking for? For each task it is important to know what the job requirements would be.

For example, for *team effectiveness*, the following behaviors should be demonstrated:

- identifying and removing barriers that keep groups or group members from working together
- listening objectively and getting input from others

- clearly explaining each person's scope of authority
- accepting responsibility for his or her choices

For *leadership and vision:*

- showing enthusiasm for organizational goals and confidence in the ability to achieve them
- holding meetings or Q&A, to solicit feedback on policies and share information on progress toward goals
- assisting individuals and groups to clearly understand organizational strategies and how they can contribute
- sponsoring forums for important information exchange at all levels

For *building relationships:*

- developing trust and keeping confidences
- soliciting and offering advice when appropriate and sharing information
- making the effort to communicate informally with others
- taking the time to meet with others to foster cooperation

For *risk-taking:*

- making tough decisions
- confronting problems promptly
- encouraging others to accept additional responsibilities and take reasonable risks
- regularly asking for help when issues arise and encouraging others to assist and suggest solutions

For *problem-solving/decision-making:*

- measuring and comparing the effectiveness of existing problem-solving models and methods
- exercising influence to reframe seemingly unsolvable problems, thereby opening up a path to solutions
- acting as a role model when personally making decisions
- thinking through failures or disappointing decisions, tracing the root cause, and taking decisive action to avoid repeating them

BEHAVIORAL QUESTIONS

Behavioral questions can be used to see the degree to which the candidate has been successful in the past, in demonstrating these job requirements/traits. A structured pattern of questions is designed to probe the individual's past behavior and accomplishments in situations similar to those that will be found in the new job.

For example, if *intellectual ability and problem-solving* were an important part of the job, the following questions might be used to assess this area:

- Tell me about a business problem you had to solve and the process you used.
- Tell me about a problem you had that required careful analysis on your part.
- Give me an example of a recent accomplishment that required you to analyze and come up with a solution.
- Give me an example of a recent business decision you made and how you went about making it. What was your process? Who was involved? What was the outcome of the decision?
- How do you solve problems?

For *team orientation:*

- Tell me about a recent situation where you had to rely on the cooperation of your peers to get a job done.
- Different people define "team" differently. What is your definition of "team" and give me an example of a recent team you were on. What was your role? How was the team formed? How were you able to balance between personal and organizational objectives?
- What is the process you use to form a team? Give me an example of a recent team that you led.

For *attention to detail:*

- Think about a recent project you were on. How did you go about getting the detail you needed to complete the project?

- What process do you use to collect data? How much data do you believe is necessary to carry out a task?
- How do you go about organizing data? Give me an example of a recent task in which you had to organize an extensive amount of data.

For *initiative:*

- How do you like to stay busy on the job? When you're not busy, what do you like to do?
- Give me an example of something you started and completed on your own. Why did you pursue this activity? What motivated you to do this extra work?
- Give me an example of a time you identified a better way to handle your daily activities or to improve some of your procedures.

THE PURPOSE

These kinds of tailored questions can also be used to understand key motivational issues that will impact a candidate on the job. For example, what kind of environment will the candidate strive in? One that is more team-oriented or one that is individual? One that is more structured or that is flexible? One that demands long hours or a regular work schedule? The key is to understand the needs of the individual, and then compare them with the needs of the organization and the job to be filled. Remember, the emphasis is on getting behavioral examples by using samples of a candidate's skills and accomplishments based on past behaviors.

The more we apply these kinds of questions the more we will move away from stereotyping, gut feelings, and biases. To do this well, it is important to evaluate people on "can they," "will they," and "fit." *Can they* show the skills and abilities required to do the job? *Will they* have the motivation and aspirations needed to do the job? Can they *fit* into the culture and values of their prospective employer?

PATTERNS

We cannot jump to the conclusion that we know what satisfies individuals until the patterns of their background are identified. Getting better and unbiased data is the key. There is no sense in hiring people who we think can or will do the job only to find out that we were snowed or duped in the process. Both the organization and the individual lose out. What people are looking for today is different from the past. Many people are looking for a balance in their lives with respect to family and business, others are looking for an opportunity to help them make a difference, while still others are looking for a job, anything that will pay them a wage.

BIAS

Bias can potentially play a big role in the interview process. Behavioral interviewing is a unique, time-tested interviewing method that minimizes bias by maximizing facts. Think about the following biases that are at work in the assessment process: the "halo effect," first impressions, stereotyping, "similar to me," "contrast effect," and the toughness bias. All six play a major role in the overall assessment of the candidate.

1. In the *halo effect*, the candidate is so impressive in one area that the interviewer ends up rating him high in all areas, or so low in one area that he is rated low in all subsequent areas.

2. In *first impressions*, a candidate makes such a good or poor first impression that the interviewer ignores what she does after that.

3. In *stereotyping*, the interviewer believes that certain groups of people are not capable of being effective employees or, conversely, that certain groups are experts in a particular technical area.

4. In the *similar to me* bias, an interviewer rates people higher if they are much like the interviewer, mistaking similarity for job ability.

5. In the *contrast effect* bias, the interviewer rates the person who is surrounded by mediocre candidates as outstanding, or rates the person who is surrounded by geniuses as inadequate because he or she looks poor in contrast.

6. In the *toughness* bias, the interviewer rates everyone at the low end of the scale.

The Common Error

All these biases contain one common error: failure to rate people solely on their qualifications as they relate to the requirements of the job. This failure effectively minimizes affirmative action, does not value differences, and does not help manage diversity. The fact is that each interviewer has his or her own biases, so it is important to understand what they are in order to minimize the effect on the assessment process. One important technique to use, when first meeting a candidate, is to acknowledge your first impression. Write it down, and by doing so you will be able to go on with the rest of the interview. If not, there may be a tendency to create that very bias that will limit an effective evaluation interview.

LEGAL DEFENSE

Behavioral interviewing is legally defensible when approached in the right manner. In lieu of giving general questions that can evoke bias and lack of interpretation, using questions that relate to the job requirements allows for better assessment and validation.

Chapter Nine

Legal Issues: Questions You Can't Ask in an Interview

![J]ob interviews, like all other phases of the selection process, should be conducted in accordance with formal, objective guidelines for evaluating a job applicant's qualifications. Motivation, ambition, interest in the trade, willingness to accept directions, and the individual's attitude toward related instruction are generally permissible subjects of pre-employment inquiries.

However, interviewers need to make sure that all pre-employment inquiries represent this kind of business necessity or job-relatedness and do not discriminate against minority group members and/or females. Failure to conduct pre-employment inquiries in a consistent, standardized manner from one job applicant to the next may invite charges of discrimination. When such charges are filed, the burden of proof is on the employer to show that all pre-employment questions are job-related and nondiscriminatory.

Many times during the course of an interview it is easy to get off track and find yourself asking questions in areas that either are not pertinent to the specific position or are just inappropriate to ask. Over the years we have attempted to capture the kinds of questions that interviewers might be interested in but may not be allowed based on equal employment law.

The following pages are based on a review of equal employment law and outline appropriate and inappropriate lines of questions in 24 key areas. While we have attempted to capture the majority of these areas, be sure if you have questions to ask an expert in workplace law.

1. Personal Information

What kinds of questions are permissible to ask relating to an applicant's name?

Appropriate: *The interviewer can inquire whether an individual has previously worked for the employer under a different name. Also, in an effort to verify work and/or educational records, employers may request former names or nicknames used by the individual.*

Inappropriate: *Non-job-related inquiries that would indicate the individual's ancestry, national origin, or descent are inappropriate. For example, "What kind of name is that?" or "What was your maiden name?"*

2. Sex

To what extent are sex inquiries unlawful?

Appropriate: *Inquiries to restrict employment because of sex are permissible only if they are "bona fide occupational qualifications" (BFOQs). For example, sex may very well be a BFOQ for reasons of authenticity (actress, actor) or moral standards (restroom attendant).*

Inappropriate: *Inquiries that ask directly about an applicant's ability to perform a certain job because of sex are inappropriate. For example, a female applicant cannot be screened out simply because a job involves physical labor or heavy lifting, nor can sex be used as a factor for determining whether the applicant will be satisfied with a particular job.*

3. Race, Ethnicity, and Other Personal Factors

What questions can be asked about race, ethnicity, and other personal factors?

Appropriate: *Federal law does not expressly prohibit questions concerning an applicant's race, color, religion, sex, national origin, or physical or mental disability, as long as they are "bona fide occupational* *qualifications" (BFOQs). Questions posed must be significantly related to successful job performance. Race and sex are not considered a reasonable basis for BFOQ. This means that if any job qualifications or selection standards have the effect of screening out women or minority groups, even though unintentional, the employer must be able to prove that (1) the standards are significantly related to job performance, and (2) no alternative nondiscriminatory standards can be developed to meet the requirements of the job. The employer must also be sure that any qualifications imposed are job-related and do not have the purpose of screening out the disabled.*

Inappropriate: *The EEOC regards with "extreme disfavor" questions concerning race, color (skin, eyes, hair, etc.), religion, sex, national origin, ancestry, marital status, and physical or mental disabilities.*

4. Marital and Family Status

What questions relating to marital status, number of children, and provisions for child care are discriminatory?

Appropriate: *Interviewers may ask questions regarding an applicant's activities, commitment, or responsibilities that could prevent him or her from meeting specified work schedules or attendance requirements. The Supreme Court has ruled that an employer must administer the same policies for men and women with pre-school children.*

Inappropriate: *Questions addressed to females about marital status, pregnancy, future child-bearing plans, and number and age of children are frequently used to deny or limit employment opportunities for female applicants. It is a violation of Title VII for employers to require information about child care arrangements from female applicants only.*

5. Pregnancy

How does the Pregnancy Discrimination Act apply to questions?

Inappropriate: *Any questions relating to pregnancy or medical history concerning pregnancy are inappropriate. The EEOC has ruled that to refuse to hire a female solely because she is pregnant amounts to sex discrimination.*

6. Age

Can an individual be asked his or her age? If so, when?

Appropriate: *This question can be acceptable when it is used as a pre-employment practice for suspected minors. Interviewers may then require proof of minimum legal working age in the form of a work permit or certificate of age. Note: the Labor Department recommends the issuance of a disclaimer stating that age will not be used in any employment decision in accordance with the Age Discrimination Act.*

Inappropriate: *It is usually difficult or impossible to prove that age is a BFOQ necessary to perform the job. It is unlawful to make inquiries designed to discover an individual's age in the form of a birth certificate during the selection process.*

7. Education

To what extent would disqualification of an applicant who does not have a high school diploma or college degree be a violation?

Appropriate: *Inquiries referring to an individual's academic or vocational education, schools attended, or his or her language skills, such as reading, speaking, and writing must be directly related to performance on the job or proven to be a job necessity.*

Inappropriate: *The Supreme Court has found an employer's requirement of a high school education discriminatory where there is no evidence that the requirement was significantly related to successful job performance. Also inappropriate are inquiries relating to the nationality, racial, or religious affiliation of the school.*

8. Experience

To what extent is experience a valid preselection inquiry?

Appropriate: *Inquiries may be made relating to an applicant's job-related work or educational or training experience only.*

Inappropriate: *Inquiries concerning an applicant's non-job-related work and/or experiences are inadvisable.*

9. Military Service

What questions can be asked about an applicant's military service?

Appropriate: *Job-related inquiries about military work experience or training gained while in the U.S. Armed Services may be made.*

Inappropriate: *Interviewers are urged not to ask questions that refer to the type of discharge an applicant received.*

10. Height and Weight

To what extent is it a violation to have height and weight requirements for a job?

Appropriate: *Employers must show that their physical standards are legitimately essential to job requirements and to the safe performance of the job in question.*

Inappropriate: *Courts and the EEOC have ruled minimum height and weight requirements to be illegal if they screen out a disproportionate number of minority group individuals or women or on the basis of handicap.*

11. Handicaps

To what extent is it a violation to inquire about handicaps or medical conditions?

Appropriate: *Inquiries regarding the ability to perform required job specifications with or without reasonable accommodation are acceptable.*

Inappropriate: *Inquiries about disability, medical history, medications, hospitalizations, and workers' compensation history are inappropriate.*

12. References

What references are permissible to request?

Appropriate: *Interviewers may request applicants to give names of character references and referral sources. Note: referrals will ordinarily be limited to term of employment, position, and salary. If more information is needed, it is advisable to get a release from the applicant.*

Inappropriate: *Interviewers should not inquire about references that would reveal the applicant's religious preferences. For example: "Can you give me the name of your clergyman as a reference?"*

13. Friends and Relatives

To what extent would it be discriminatory to ask an applicant whether he or she has friends and/or relatives working for the company?

Appropriate: *Inquiries should be restricted to questions that can be justified as business necessity or job-related. Some companies may not have rules against hiring relatives, but all hiring must be based on qualifications and not relationships.*

Inappropriate: *Requesting such information might be unlawful if it indicates a preference for friends and relatives of present employees, and if the composition of the present work force is such that this preference would reduce or eliminate opportunities for women or minority group members, where underrepresentation exists. Such information is not relevant to an applicant's competence.*

14. Economic Status

To what extent would it be a violation to make inquiries relating to an applicant's financial status?

Appropriate: *Unless business necessity can be shown, no inquiries are permissible. If credit checks are necessary, they must comply strictly with the Fair Credit Reporting Act.*

Inappropriate: *Questions concerning credit rating, garnishment records, bankruptcy, charge accounts, car ownership, length of residence at an address, and rental or ownership of a house could constitute violations of Title VII if used to make employment decisions. For example: "How is your credit rating?" or "Have you ever had your pay garnished?"*

15. Citizenship

To what extent is it permissible to ask an applicant whether he or she is a U.S. citizen?

Appropriate: *Under the Immigration Control Act of 1986, you are required to ascertain that all new hires are legally entitled to work in the United States. During the interview, you can mention that, if hired, all applicants must submit proof of a right to work in the United States.*

Inappropriate: *Interviewers should not ask applicants about the country of their origin, whether their parents or spouse are naturalized or native-born U.S. citizens, or the date when the applicant, spouse, and/or parents acquired U.S. citizenship.*

16. National Origin

To what extent is "national origin" an acceptable question?

Appropriate: *Inquiries may be made into the applicant's ability to read, write, and speak English or foreign languages when required for a specific job.*

Inappropriate: *Questions about the applicant's lineage, ancestry, national origin, descent, place of birth, national origin of parents or spouse, or how the applicant acquired the ability to read, write, or speak a foreign language are all inappropriate.*

17. Religion

To what extent can inquiries be made concerning an applicant's religious preference or his or her availability to work on Saturdays, Sundays, or holidays?

Appropriate: *Employers must set forth the schedule and then inquire if there are any scheduling conflicts. If there are conflicts, then Title VII requires that employers make "reasonable accommodation" for "a prospective employee's religious observance," unless it causes "undue economic hardship." When such inquiries are made, the interviewer should let the applicant know that a reasonable effort will be made to accommodate any religious needs should he or she be hired.*

Inappropriate: *Such inquiries should not be made when a business necessity or job-relatedness cannot be proven. Also, inquiries should not be made about an applicant's religious denomination, religious affiliation, church, parish, pastor, or religious holidays observed.*

18. Arrest

To what extent is it discriminatory to make arrest inquiries to disqualify applicants?

Inappropriate: *The Court and the EEOC have held that an employer's use of an arrest record to disqualify applicants is unlawful. For example, "Have you ever been in trouble with the law?" or "Have you ever been arrested?"*

19. Conviction

To what extent can an interviewer use conviction inquiries to disqualify applicants?

Appropriate: *An applicant's criminal record may be considered when he or she has been convicted of a job-related crime within five years of the date of application and the conviction relates to job duties, or when business necessity can be proven.*

Inappropriate: *A U.S. District Court has held that an applicant's criminal record should not be considered for a crime committed over five years prior to the date of application for the job.*

20. Residence

When are questions relating to residence acceptable?

Appropriate: *Inquiries may be made about the applicant's address if it is needed for future contact with the applicant.*

Inappropriate: *Inquiries about whether the applicant owns or rents his or her home and/or names or relationships of persons with whom the applicant resides, are inappropriate. For example, "Who else do you live with?" or "Do you live with your family?"*

21. Organizations

To what extent is an employer in violation when an applicant's organizational affiliation is asked?

Appropriate: *Inquiries of this nature should be avoided unless proven to be job-related or a business necessity; that is, for example, you may* *inquire whether the applicant for an engineering job belongs to an engineering organization.*

Inappropriate: *Inquiries about organizations, clubs, societies, and lodges whose name or character indicates members' economic or social class, race, color, sex, marital status, religion, or ancestry, such as country clubs and/or fraternal orders, are inappropriate.*

22. Photographs

At what time is an employer permitted to request a photograph?

Appropriate: *It is permissible for an employer to require a photograph for identification only after hiring.*

Inappropriate: *Applicants should not be required to submit a photograph either before or after an interview is conducted.*

23. Drug/Alcohol Use

To what extent can you ask questions regarding drug and alcohol use?

Appropriate: *An employer can provide information as to corporate policy and expectations with which all employees are required to comply.*

Inappropriate: *Inquiries cannot be made regarding whether a person uses medications, alcohol, or other drugs.*

24. Attendance

To what extent can you ask about the use of sick leave and/or attendance at prior employment?

Appropriate: *An employer can provide corporate policy regarding sick leave and attendance and ask the applicant if he or she would have conflicts that would prevent compliance.*

Inappropriate: *Inquiries cannot be made about reasons for absence, use of sick leave, or extent of use of sick leave.*

Part Three

Interpreting the Candidate's Responses

Chapter Ten
How to Interpret Responses in an Interview

I n the next several chapters of this book, emphasis swings from securing information to interpreting findings. Interpreting information is just as important as securing it. Because of the interdependence of the two, however, no effort will be made to confine the discussion to interpretation alone. In fact, subsequent chapters will be concerned with the specifics of exploring and interpreting each major area of the interview. Prior to any discussion of information obtained from the various interview areas, some consideration must be given to the interpretation process itself.

COMPLEXITIES OF INTERPRETATION

Interview data is not made up of cold, hard facts that can be reduced to any precise mathematical formula. For the most part, it is composed of clues that alert the interviewer to the possible existence of certain traits of personality and motivation. The interview produces a large mass of information, only part of which is relevant in terms of interpretation. As the discussion proceeds, the interviewer has to make decisions about what is relevant and what is not.

A given candidate's qualifications comprise a relatively large number of individual traits and abilities. Interview data must therefore be obtained and organized in such a way that there is sufficient supporting information for evaluating each of the requisite characteristics. It is not enough to know that the candidate has had sufficient technical training and experience; the interviewer must also decide the extent to which that candidate possesses such characteristics as honesty, willingness to work, ability to get along with others, emotional stability, self-confidence, and ability to plan and organize. Despite the complexities of evaluation, experience has nevertheless shown that, within a few days, appropriately qualified individuals can be trained to interpret interview findings with a relatively high degree of accuracy.

FIRST CONSIDERATIONS

Since there is no point in interpreting information we do not believe or cannot take at face value, we must first try to determine whether or not a candidate is telling the truth and whether or not the individual's standards are unrealistically high or low. Although answers to these two questions may not be obtained until the interview is perhaps half over, it seems logical to treat these two factors here before getting involved with interpretation per se.

How to Determine if a Candidate Is Telling the Truth

There are at least three valid means of determining the extent to which a candidate may be telling the truth: (1) internal consistency, (2) the amount of unfavorable information a candidate provides, and (3) an obvious tendency to exaggerate accomplishments. By "internal consistency," we mean consistency of information between the two major areas of the interview, work history and education. If an individual is immature, evidence of this should appear in both of these major areas. It would be most unlikely, for example, that a candidate would reflect a high degree of maturity as a part of her or his work history, but a low degree of maturity with respect to education. If such a situation should occur, the interviewer should immediately suspect that the person might not be telling the truth.

The same would be true the other way around. A candidate, for example, might reflect immaturity by mentioning unsound reasons for leaving jobs, poorly thought-out vocational goals, or aspirations way out of line with his abilities. In order for the discussion of education to be internally consistent, this same candidate might be expected to reveal such clues to immaturity as studying hard on only those courses he liked, rationalizing failures by blaming teachers or the school system, or selecting a major course of study with no thought as to how that major might be used after getting out of school. It is when the data become inconsistent that the interviewer should begin to question the candidate's story. Thus, if the candidate cited above claimed that he did his homework every single evening, studied a lot harder on the courses that he did not like in order to get good grades, or never cut any classes, the interviewer might begin to feel he was telling us what he thought we wanted to hear rather than what actually happened.

On the other hand, when candidates appear to be on the level and provide a fair amount of unfavorable information along with the more favorable data, this may also be regarded as evidence that they are telling the truth. If, for example, a female candidate admits that she was fired from a given job, that her attendance was not all that good, or that her typing speed is only 30 words a minute, the interviewer gets the feeling she is telling us her life story just as it actually occurred. With such a candidate, therefore, considerable credence can be placed in statements about achievements.

Some candidates have a rather strong tendency to exaggerate their achievements, and this is quite easily picked up. In discussing outside interests, for example, a woman might claim that she reads four or five books a week. If that same woman had indicated a dislike of verbal subjects such as English, foreign languages, and history, her claim of reading four or five books a week would be internally inconsistent and probably an exaggeration. Likewise, a man who claims never to have spoken a word in anger strikes us as too good to be true and is probably exaggerating.

As we shall see, however, candidates' characteristics should not be judged on single clues. Rather, the interviewer should try to develop a series of clues before making a judgment on a characteristic as important as honesty. How to develop this kind of documentation is the subject of the three chapters on interpretation.

It may seem to some that no candidate would be likely to provide some of the negative information indicated above, but that is simply not true. When interviewers are successful in developing rapport and getting spontaneous information, they find themselves regularly obtaining information of a negative character that is surprising even to them.

Unrealistic Personal Standards

Even when the interviewer believes that candidates are telling the truth, not all their comments are taken at face value when it can be determined that their personal standards are unrealistically high or low. When asked to tell about his shortcomings, a candidate, for example, might indicate that he "probably should work a little harder." This might seem completely inconsistent if the interviewer has already developed a considerable amount of hard data supporting a willingness to work very hard. The interviewer may then suspect that the candidate's professed shortcoming stems from his tendency to be a perfectionist and hence to feel that he never does anything as well as he should. In such cases, interviewers rely upon accumulated hard data (clues to willingness to work hard picked up through the discussion of work history and education) rather than upon candidates' statements regarding their shortcomings.

Personal standards may also indicate seeming inconsistencies at the other end of the spectrum. When asked to indicate her strengths, a woman, for example, may claim to be a hard worker when all the hard data indicate that just the opposite may be the case. But the inconsistency here may be based upon low personal standards rather than upon dishonesty. Some people's standards are so low that it does not take much to satisfy them. Hence, they may think of themselves as hard workers when this is actually not the case at all.

Fortunately, the hard data (clues to behavior) usually turn out to be consistent with a candidate's own assessment of his or her abilities. Inconsistencies that are due to unrealistically high or low personal standards will not be frequent, but they should be identified as such when they do occur.

PROCESS OF INTERPRETATION

As one might expect, it is easier to train interviewers to secure the necessary information than it is to train them to interpret the findings. It requires a fair amount of analytical ability, not only to recognize clues to behavior but also to catalog such clues in terms of assets and shortcomings. As the discussion progresses, the interviewer must constantly separate the wheat from the chaff, searching for clues to such characteristics as willingness to work, ability to get along with others, emotional maturity, and leadership potential.

Interpretation as an Ongoing Process

Interviewers who wait until the end of the interview to decide what they think of a candidate are hopelessly lost. The interpretation process, in fact, begins as soon as candidates enter the room and continues until they leave. Clues to behavior build throughout the interview, so that a candidate's overall qualifications normally become quite evident by the time the interview has been concluded. Interviewers who do a good ongoing job of interpretation should know whether or not they want to hire the individual by the time that person leaves the room. In interviewing more and more people, interviewers build up a frame of reference that enables them to compare the qualifications of a given candidate with those of all the other people they have recently seen.

Interviewers Learn to Mask Their Reactions

As the candidate's story unfolds, interviewers mentally scrutinize each bit of information for possible clues to behavior. Yet they carry out this evaluation process in such a way that they completely mask their true reaction and hence do not give the candidate the slightest inkling of how they are interpreting a remark. To do otherwise might risk loss of rapport. An interviewer who registers surprise or disapproval as a result of uncovering unfavorable information frequently turns candidates off to the point where the interviewer never succeeds in getting them to open up again.

Cataloging Clues

As soon as a candidate enters the room, interviewers should begin to get impressions of that individual in terms of possible effectiveness in the job for which he or she is being considered. It may be noted, for example, that a candidate presents a nice appearance and has an appreciable amount of poise and presence—clues that may be catalogued mentally as factors in the person's possible effectiveness with people.

As the interview progresses, the interviewer may become impressed with the complete candor with which the candidate discusses strengths and shortcomings and may catalog that as an indication of sincerity and maturity. (Individuals who know themselves in terms of their strengths and limitations are often more mature than their chronological age group.) Later on, the candidate may indicate that he or she often stays on after quitting time in order to get a job done or even comes in on a Saturday. The interviewer catalogs this, naturally, as a clue to conscientiousness and willingness to work. And so it goes throughout the interview. Each statement the candidate makes is carefully examined in terms of its implied as well as its obvious meaning. Resulting clues to behavior are then mentally catalogued as possible indications of such traits as initiative, perseverance, emotional adjustment, adaptability, and leadership potential.

Relevance of Candidate's Work History and Education

Interviewers look not only for clues to behavior but also for the extent to which a candidate's previous experience and training have provided adequate preparation for the position in question. If the job in question, for example, involves excessive detail, interviewers should be quick to note any previous detail-oriented experience and how the individual reacted to this. They know full well that individuals who have already experienced this kind of work know what they are getting into and adapt to it much more readily than someone without such experience.

Mentally Organize a List of Assets and Liabilities

As the discussion progresses, interviewers mentally compile a list of the candidate's strengths and shortcomings. Although their outward manner is permissive and disarming, they nevertheless evaluate analytically and critically everything a candidate has to say. As the interview progresses from work history to education and finally to outside interests, a general pattern of behavior normally begins to make itself evident.

Interviewers may get clue after clue attesting to a candidate's forcefulness, willingness to accept responsibility, and strong drive to get things done quickly. At the same time, a high degree of strength in certain areas may be accompanied by concomitant shortcomings in other areas. Interviewers may also pick up a series of clues indicating lack of tact, inflexibility, or even ruthlessness. As they catalog such clues, they find it increasingly possible to build a list of assets and liabilities. In fact, such a list of assets and liabilities should be so well documented by the end of the discussion that interviewers can write them down immediately after the candidate leaves the room. At that point, interviewers make the hiring decision on the basis of the extent to which the assets outweigh the liabilities or vice versa.

Searching for Clues to Intelligence

In addition to the search for personality traits and the relevance of previous experience and training, interviewers also look for the level of the candidate's basic abilities. As noted in Chapter 3, aptitude tests can be of tremendous help in establishing the level of a candidate's mental, verbal, and numerical ability, clerical aptitude, and mechanical comprehension. However, such test results are often not available, and in such cases interviewers must do the best they can to establish ability levels on the basis of their own findings. Specific suggestions for accomplishing this task will be found in subsequent chapters. Suffice it to say here, though, that some of the best clues to mental ability will be found in such factors as (1) level of grades in terms of effort required to get those grades, (2) standardized test scores, such as the SAT and GRE, and (3) a candidate's ability to respond to the more difficult depth questions.

What to Interpret

As indicated earlier, every interview results in both relevant and irrelevant information. Actually, much of what the candidate may have to say is likely to be descriptive, providing little in the way of clues to behavior. Interviewers, of course, try to keep such information to a minimum, controlling the discussion so that candidates concentrate on evaluative data. Even so, a certain amount of descriptive information is certain to ensue. Interviewers naturally pay as little attention as possible to such irrelevant data, constantly identifying the important information and making their interpretations accordingly.

The more relevant information is likely to be found in candidates' attitudes and reactions. Interviewers learn much more about people as a result of their attitudes and reactions toward a given job than from a description of the job duties. Attitudes and reactions often provide specific clues to such important factors as initiative, empathy, ability to organize, and self-confidence.

Since interviewers are also looking for the relevance of candidates' work experience and education in terms of the job for which they are being considered, interviewers must carry a mental picture of the job specifications into the discussion with them. When listening to the description of previous jobs, for example, the interviewer must be quick to notice any similarity between those jobs and the job for which the candidate is being considered. He or she must also decide whether candidates are capable of performing the job in question with minimum orientation, or whether a protracted training period will be necessary to bring them to a productive level.

How to Interpret

We have talked above about the importance of determining the relevance of a candidate's work history and education. This is a relatively simple task. One has only to compare what candidates have done in the past with what they may be expected to do in the future. What is required is an ability to get information and a clear picture of the demands of the job. Understanding and utilizing the process of contrast will help immeasurably in carrying out this interpretative function.

Contrasting the Candidate with the Job Description. This process involves the continual contrasting of each aspect of a candidate's job and school history with the specifications of the job under consideration. In those areas where little or no contrast is involved—or where the difference is in a positive direction—no real adjustment problem exists. This represents a favorable finding. On the other hand, where the contrast is appreciable, candidates might be expected to experience a very real adjustment problem in acclimating to the new job situation. Although the difference may be insufficient to exclude candidates from further consideration, such a difference nevertheless represents an unfavorable factor.

Let us assume, for example, that a given job calls for work of a highly confining nature. Candidates who have done confining work as a part of their previous experience—and who have apparently been able to accept it quite readily as part of the job—might be expected to be able to adjust to the new job much more easily than candidates without such experience. With the former group the contrast would not appear to be very great, while with the latter group the contrast would in all likelihood be significant.

Another such unfavorable contrast would be found in candidates who are already earning more money on their present job than what they would be paid as a starting salary on the new job. They might express a willingness to take the new job at a lower salary because it may offer greater long-range opportunity. Once they have been on the job for a while, however, a certain amount of dissatisfaction is likely to develop. Many such individuals decide they can't wait for future salary increases and begin looking for another job. If, on the other hand, candidates are to be paid a starting salary in excess of their present earnings, they can be expected to be more satisfied with their new lot, other things being equal. This represents something positive from the candidate's perspective, and the interviewer can evaluate this as a favorable factor.

The kind of close supervision involved in previous jobs and in a proposed new assignment may also provide an unfavorable contrast. A secretary who has had previous experience running an office and taking care of much of the correspondence might become quickly dissatisfied in a new job where every single piece of correspondence was dictated and where everything was very closely supervised. When such individuals take new positions involving much closer supervision and much less opportunity to exercise their own initiative, they normally find adjustment somewhat difficult. The alert interviewer recognizes the potentially unfavorable contrast and adds this to the list of negative factors.

Interpretation by Direct Observation. Valid judgments can be made about people simply by observing them directly. Interviewers, therefore, find it quite easy to evaluate such obvious characteristics as appearance, poise, presence, grooming, and self-expression. They simply observe a candidate's outward behavior during the discussion and make their judgments on these characteristics.

However, interpretation by direct observation is limited to the more obvious or easy-to-evaluate characteristics. It is of very little use in determining the more important factors such as honesty, judgment, intelligence, and perseverance. Yet, interpretation by direct observation is the only means available to most untrained interviewers. This is why the interview has often fared so poorly when subjected to validation studies.

Interpretation by Inference. Since interpretation by direct observation represents a relatively limited device, what method do we use to evaluate the more important characteristics? We use a time-tested method called interpretation by inference. By definition, this means that we infer from a series of clues the extent to which an individual possesses a given trait or ability. The phrase "series of clues" in this definition is extremely important since it would be most unfair and inaccurate to base an evaluation on a single unfavorable situation.

Even if a person admits to having been fired from a given job, that, in itself, would not represent an adequate basis for assuming the person was a troublemaker or a poor worker. It is conceivable, in fact, that the supervisor may have been at fault. But, if there are problems on other jobs, or if the person talks disparagingly about co-workers or about students he or she had job training with, for example, we can determine with some assurance that this individual is not able to get along with people very well. This assurance stems from the fact that we have developed a series of clues rather than having based our evaluation on a single happenstance. And, because these clues have spanned two areas of the interview—work history and education—we have established a pattern of internal consistency. When an individual has any given trait in some abundance, clues to such a trait will not be limited to a single area of the interview. Rather, such clues will surface in both the work history and education.

As indicated earlier, clues must be interpreted as soon as they become evident. This provides interviewers with a starting point on which they can build later. Using such a clue as a temporary supposition, they mentally catalog it as a possible indication of a given trait. With this supposition as a foundation, they subsequently probe at appropriate intervals throughout the discussion for additional specific clues to support the supposition.

An interviewer, for example, might obtain an early clue to immaturity, thus providing a temporary supposition; however, if no clues to immaturity become evident in a candidate's history over the 10 most recent years, the interviewer would have to throw out the initial hypothesis. On the other hand, some people never seem to grow up. Evidence may show that job-hopping, chronic dissatisfaction with practically every job, and poor judgment are still deeply rooted in an individual's behavior. In such a case, there is ample evidence—in the form of many clues pointing in the same direction—to eliminate the candidate from further consideration. We therefore see that interpretation by inference goes on throughout the interview, the interviewer making tentative hypotheses and probing specifically for confirming evidence.

Look for Leads. Since the final interview is preceded by such employment steps as the application form, the preliminary interview, and the aptitude tests, it represents an ideal opportunity to follow up on some of the leads that may have emerged from some of those early steps. Such leads often give the interviewer a tremendous head start as far as the interpretive process is concerned.

Trait Description. If we are to rate a given candidate on a series of traits, our understanding of the meaning of these traits must be as clear as possible. Psychologists themselves find it difficult to agree specifically on the definition of many traits of personality, motivation, and character. The definitions that appear below are by no means absolute, but they do provide insight into what is professionally accepted, and should therefore be of assistance to the employment interviewer.

- **Emotional maturity:** the ability to behave as an adult, to take the bitter with the sweet, to face up to failure without rationalizing or passing the buck, to acquire self-insight, to establish reasonable vocational goals, and to exercise self-control.

- **Assertiveness:** aggressiveness in social situations, leading to a strong impact of one's personality upon other people—not to be confused with drive to get a job done.

- **Tough-mindedness:** boldness to make difficult decisions involving people for the good of the organization, to stand up for what one thinks is right and not to shrink from confrontations with others when necessary.

- **Social sensitivity:** awareness of the reactions of others; judgment in social situations.

- **Conscientiousness:** willingness to put in additional time and effort on a given task in order to complete it in accordance with one's personal standards.

- **Self-discipline:** ability to carry out the less pleasant tasks without undue procrastination.

- **Initiative:** being a self-starter; willingness to try new methods, to provide one's own motivation without undue prompting from superiors.

- **Analytical capacity:** ability to break down a given problem into its component parts in a logical, systematic manner.

- **Ability to plan and organize:** ability to lay out a given task in logical sequence, approaching first things first in a systematic manner, planning future steps in such a way as to accomplish the whole task efficiently and thoroughly.

- **Critical thinking:** ability to dig down deeply in order to get to the bottom of problems, to probe beneath the surface in order to test the findings in terms of one's own experience; not to take things at face value.

- **Self-confidence:** willingness to take action based upon a realistic assessment of one's own abilities.
- **Emotional adjustment:** ability to stand up under pressure, to take a reasonably cheerful outlook on life, to be at peace with oneself.
- **Being a team worker:** willingness to do one's share of the work, ability to get along with other members of the team, willingness to subordinate one's ego to the extent that one does not try to become the "star" of the team or to claim too much credit for the joint accomplishment.

<table>
<tr><td>Chapter
Eleven</td><td># Interpreting a Candidate's Work History</td></tr>
</table>

Candidates' work histories ordinarily represent a major portion of their life's experience and, as such, not only provide an indication of their ability to do a certain job but also supply many clues as to how they will do it. The manner in which a person works is often the best single source of information concerning personality strengths and weaknesses. It is fitting, then, that candidates be encouraged to give a rather exhaustive account of their work background, particularly as it pertains to items listed under work experience in the Interview Guide. In this chapter, we will offer suggestions for structuring discussion of the work history. This will be followed by an item-by-item discussion of factors listed under "work experience" on the Interview Guide (see Appendix A).

HOW TO STRUCTURE DISCUSSION OF WORK HISTORY

The reader will recall that, in the effort to get candidates talking spontaneously, the discussion of all major areas of the interview begins with a comprehensive lead question. In launching the work history discussion, interviewers may use such a comprehensive question as

"Suppose you start by telling me about your work experience, beginning with your first job and working up to the present. I would like to
know how you got each job, what you did, your likes, dislikes, earnings,
and so forth. Where do we start? Did you have any jobs while attending high school?"

In talking about various jobs, candidates will normally provide
spontaneous information concerning many of the factors listed under
"work history" on the Interview Guide. When they fail to provide such
information—or if they do not discuss important factors in sufficient
detail—interviewers should prompt them by appropriately worded follow-up questions and comments.

Remember, too, that the work history should be kept pure, in the
sense that the interviewer encourages candidates to concentrate on
jobs, without supplying much information about other interview areas.
When candidates begin to ramble or to provide too much descriptive
information, the interviewer controls the situation by interrupting them
with a carefully timed compliment and bringing them back to the subject under discussion.

As a candidate relates his job history, the interviewer mentally
checks this experience against job description and behavior specifications of the job under consideration. The fewer adjustments and adap-
tations individuals have to make in moving from previous jobs to a new
job, the more likely they are to find the new job satisfying and the more
quickly they should be able to make a meaningful contribution.

Duties

Candidates should not be permitted to devote too much time to a
description of job duties, particularly in the case of the initial jobs.
When they get to their more important experiences, however, they
should be encouraged to talk in some detail about what they actually
did on these jobs. For the most part, interviewers do not expect candidates to have performed duties that are exactly the same as those they
will be responsible for in a new job. Rather, they evaluate the general
nature of candidates' experiences, assuming that they should be able
to carry out new duties that are generally similar to what they have

done in the past. In hiring an engineer for the design of automatic control systems for jet engines, it may not be absolutely necessary to find someone whose previous experience has been devoted to jet engines. If the candidate has successfully designed automatic-control systems for other highly technical power plants, such as those concerned with guided missiles or torpedoes, he or she should be able to assume design responsibilities on jet-engine control systems without too much orientation.

Information concerning the duties of the candidate's more important jobs also tells the interviewer about the degree of responsibility the candidate has handled. Such responsibility may have been highly technical or it may have involved the supervision of other people. In either case, the interviewer needs to know the degree of responsibility assumed, the exact nature of the technical duties, or the number of persons supervised. To get specific information, the interviewer may have to interrupt the candidate's story from time to time. As the candidate goes from one job to another, the interviewer has an opportunity to note the progress in assuming responsibility. Such progress—or the lack of it—may provide clues to the individual's general ability.

Where considerable progress has been made, the interviewer will probe for the why—those specific traits and abilities that have been responsible for the individual's success. Where lack of progress is evident, the interviewer will be equally interested in trying to find the underlying reasons. In the latter case, particular note will be taken of any attempt on a candidate's part to rationalize failures, as a possible clue to immaturity.

When interviewers encounter people who have made unusual progress, they should use the following question: "What traits do you think you demonstrated that caused your supervisors to move you ahead so rapidly?" This usually results in responses such as "I worked very hard" or "I was very reliable; I never missed a day" or "I got along very well with people." It is a good idea to probe further here: "What other traits were responsible for your progress?"

Likes

Since attitudes and reactions to a particular job experience normally tell us much more about people than a recitation of job duties, a great deal of attention should be devoted to likes and dislikes. If candidates omit this from their discussion, they should be reminded by such a follow-up question as "What were some of the things you liked best on that job?"

Moreover, interviewers should not be satisfied with a single response. They should probe for additional "likes." Likes on previous jobs can supply many clues to abilities, personality traits, and motivation. Someone who has shown a liking for responsibility—particularly where people are concerned—may have a certain degree of initiative and leadership ability. Someone who derives particular satisfaction from contacts with workers in the shop may possess a considerable amount of common touch. Likes and abilities tend to be fairly highly correlated, in the sense that we tend to do best on those tasks we enjoy most. For example, a liking for mathematics may indicate that the individual has a fair amount of aptitude for mathematically oriented work.

But likes are equally valuable in providing clues to possible shortcomings. The woman who liked a job because of its regular hours, frequent vacations, and lack of overtime work may be the kind of person who does not like to extend herself by putting in extra effort on a job. If this can be supported by subsequent clues pointing in the same direction, the interviewer will have come up with an important finding concerning the woman's lack of motivation.

Thus likes may provide clues to both assets and shortcomings. Someone who enjoyed a given job because she had a good deal of freedom may be saying that she is the kind of person who, on the one hand, likes responsibility but, on the other hand, tends to be overly independent. In response to such a finding, then, the interviewer would do some two-step probing in an effort to find out what there was about having a completely free hand that gave the individual so much satisfaction.

Dislikes

Having had a chance to discuss likes in considerable detail, the candidate is normally quite willing to talk about dislikes, particularly if good rapport has been established. At the same time, the interviewer should approach this subject adroitly by softening the follow-up question. Instead of asking about a person's dislikes, he should pose such a question as "What were some of the things you found less satisfying on that job?" It is possible that a candidate may not have any actual job dislikes in a particular situation, but, considered relatively, there are always some aspects of a job that are less satisfying than others. In the event that the candidate is able to come up with very little in the way of things that were less appealing to her, the interviewer should stimulate the discussion by means of a laundry-list question. He can say, "What were some of the other things that were less appealing on that job—were they concerned with the earnings, the type of supervision you received, the amount of detail involved, or perhaps the lack of opportunity to use your own initiative?"

If the interviewer has previously formed an initial hypothesis about certain possible shortcomings, he will include pertinent items in the laundry-list question. Thus if he suspects laziness, he might include such an item as "or an overly demanding supervisor" in the laundry-list question as one of the possible job factors the individual may have found less satisfying.

Remember, too, that probing for job dislikes often results in spontaneous information as to why the person eventually left the job. If such information can be obtained indirectly and spontaneously, the real truth of the matter is more likely to be elicited. The candidate may say, for example, "I just couldn't see eye to eye with my supervisor, and quite frankly that was why I left." In such a situation, the interviewer would naturally play this down and probe deeper by saying, "Some bosses are certainly very hard to get along with. What was your boss's particular problem?"

Information concerning job dissatisfactions can provide a wide variety of clues to the individual's possible shortcomings. He may admit, for example, that the mathematical calculations aspect of his job represented a factor of dissatisfaction, and he may further disclose the fact that he does not consider himself particularly qualified in this area. The interviewer would then have a strong clue to lack of mathematical aptitude. If test scores are available and if they show below-average numerical ability, the interview finding in this case would confirm the results of the test.

Another candidate may volunteer the information that she disliked being left on her own so much of the time without much direction from above, which might provide a clue to lack of confidence and a tendency to be dependent upon others. In another job situation, the candidate may reveal that the assignment was not sufficiently well structured. This may indicate a clue to the inability to plan and organize, as well as a possible lack of initiative. Still another may complain about the fact that he was required to juggle too many balls in the air at one time, which might point to a possible lack of flexibility and adaptability or a lack of general mental ability. In any event, the interviewer carefully catalogues such clues and looks subsequently for supporting data.

Discussion of job dislikes can also reveal clues to assets. In fact, the very willingness to talk about dislikes frequently provides clues to honesty, sincerity, and self-confidence. In supplying negative information, the individual in a sense says, "This is the way I am constituted; if you don't have a place for me here, I am confident of my ability to locate something somewhere else." When a candidate discusses negative information candidly and objectively, the interviewer soon comes to the conclusion that she is getting the complete story, and she gives the person credit for being honest and sincere.

Working Conditions

People who have become conditioned to hard work and long hours in the past can be expected to apply themselves with like diligence in the future. Particularly when they have found it necessary to extend themselves by working 60 or 70 hours a week or by going to school at night while carrying on a full-time job during the day, they normally develop a greater capacity for constructive effort than might otherwise have been the case. A young woman who works after school and during summers while going to high school and college normally develops work habits that stand her in good stead later on. On the other hand, the college graduate who has never worked at all may be expected to find adjustment to the first post-college job somewhat difficult. Of course, such individuals should not be excluded from further consideration because of lack of any kind of work experience, but this should nevertheless be included in the overall evaluation as a possibly unfavorable factor.

As the candidate talks about working conditions on previous jobs, the interviewer should mentally compare such conditions with specifications of the job for which he is being evaluated. If the job requires working under pressure, for example, the interviewer will look specifically for any previous jobs carried out by the candidate where pressure was an important factor. In addition, she will try to get the subject's reaction to such pressure. If an individual found it hard to work under pressure and even includes this as a reason for leaving a particular job, his qualifications for the new job would be viewed with some question. Or, if the new job is fast-moving and requires quick changes of reference, the interviewer would look specifically for previous exposure of the candidate to situations of this kind. If he has enjoyed and been stimulated by such working conditions in the past, this would obviously represent a definite asset. Today, it becomes an increasingly important asset as companies restructure and assign employees to new responsibilities.

In an earlier chapter of this book, we discussed the value of not tipping one's hand—getting the information from the candidate before giving information about the job. This is especially true with respect to working conditions. If the individual really wants the proposed assignment, she will hardly be inclined to express dissatisfaction about certain job factors that she knows exist in the position for which she is applying.

Working conditions also include the degree of supervision to which individuals have become accustomed. Here again, using the job specifications as a base, the interviewer should try to determine the extent to which the type of supervision may be expected to represent an adjustment factor, in terms of the contrast between the degree of supervision to which candidates have become accustomed and the supervision they would encounter on the proposed assignment. People who have grown accustomed to relatively little supervision on past jobs—where they have ordered their own lives, laid out their own work, and made many of their own decisions—will ordinarily chafe under close supervision in a subsequent job situation.

Obviously, they are not excluded from further consideration on this basis alone, but it nevertheless represents a negative factor. The type of supervision under which people worked in the past may provide clues to possible abilities and personality characteristics. If they have operated successfully without close supervision, for example, they may be the type of people who have a good bit of initiative and who have so much ability that their supervisors trust them to carry out day-to-day tasks without checking up on them very frequently. Moreover, natural leaders are normally people who like to work without close supervision. They enjoy the degree of responsibility that such a situation permits. And they derive satisfaction from an opportunity to exercise their own initiative.

Level of Earnings

Interviewers should get candidates in the habit of talking about earnings by asking them to give this information on early jobs. Since few people object to talking about the salary they made on jobs some years ago, they willingly supply these facts. If, moreover, they are encouraged to give salary information on each job, they provide salary figures on their most recent experience pretty much as a matter of course. On the other hand, if interviewers wait for the most recent job experience before asking about earnings, candidates may try to fence with them. A question such as "What happened to your earnings on that job in terms of starting and ending compensation?" usually proves quite efficient.

The pattern of earnings over the years represents one important criterion of the individual's job progress to date. In cases in which the candidate's earnings have gone up rather quickly, it can usually be assumed that she is a person of some ability. In cases like this, the interviewer will want to probe for the reasons why the individual has done so well, since such probing may provide clues to her major assets. Again, the question, "What traits did you demonstrate that caused your supervisor to raise your salary so handsomely?" will often result in valuable information. On the other hand, earnings are not always a true reflection of ability. A man may have been in the right place at the right time, may have been given special treatment because his father was a partial owner of the company, or may have been successful in impressing his superiors on the basis of his persuasive personality rather than because of his real ability.

Just as a rapid rise in earnings normally points to the existence of assets, so does lack of salary progress frequently reflect a series of significant shortcomings. A candidate in her middle 30s who has shown relatively little salary progress in the last 10 years is usually lacking in ability, effectiveness of personality, or motivation. In probing for the reasons, however, the interviewer may find that the candidate has been confronted with circumstances somewhat beyond her control. He may find that the individual has been working in a relatively low-paying field such as the utilities industry, or that she has been reluctant to give up the security of that particular job because of the serious illness of a family member.

In probing for the real reasons, the interviewer should obviously avoid such a direct question as "How do you account for your failure to earn more money over the years?" Rather, he should approach this situation more indirectly, bringing up the question under the discussion of job dislikes. If the candidate does not mention salary as a factor of dissatisfaction, the interviewer can say, "How do you feel about your salary? Are you relatively satisfied with what you are making, or do you think that your job merits somewhat more?" The subsequent response may indicate a number of interesting clues to behavior, including lack of salary aspirations, bitterness over lack of salary progress, rationalization of the situation, or general recognition of shortcomings and willingness to accept her lot in life.

In evaluating salary progress, one should keep the level of the individual's basic abilities in mind. If a person is bright mentally and has good general abilities, lack of salary aspirations may point to inadequate motivation. In the case of an individual who is somewhat limited intellectually but has nevertheless been moved along rapidly, subsequent frustration will almost certainly occur if and when such progress comes to a halt. Such a person has become accustomed to rapid promotion and hence expects this pattern to be maintained. In the case of the overachiever, the time will undoubtedly come when mental limitations will preclude further promotion, at which time the person will probably become a most unhappy individual. On the other hand, a mentally limited individual who has learned to accept such limitations and not to expect too much has usually attained an admirable degree of emotional maturity.

Performance Appraisal

Many managers do an inadequate job of rating the performance of those reporting to them and an even poorer job of feeding back the results to the individuals involved. Even so, it is often fruitful to ask candidates about their performance appraisals on important jobs. After discussing duties, likes, dislikes, and earnings, probe for appraisal results, first getting the overall rating (excellent, above average, average, or below average) and subsequently asking about strengths and indicated development needs.

Always ask about strengths first: "What were the traits or abilities your supervisor said she liked about you?" Then: "What other traits did she like?" After you have been able to develop information about several strengths, switch to the discussion of development needs: "What traits or abilities did she think needed a little more development?" If, as in so many cases, the supervisor did not discuss any shortcomings, say, "Well, what traits do you think you could have improved?" Do not ask about performance appraisals on every single job or this will become redundant and will detract from the importance of the discussion of the overall strengths and development needs, which takes place at the end of the work history.

In most cases, the information gleaned from the discussion of performance appraisals tends to be quite consistent and provides interviewers with important findings concerning candidates' motivation, mental ability, and maturity. And this information also gives them a storehouse of data from which they can "prime the pump" in helping candidates subsequently to discuss their overall strengths and shortcomings.

Reasons for Changing Jobs

This is one of the most delicate aspects of the interview, since many candidates are sensitive about their reasons for having left certain jobs. Therefore, we try to get this information spontaneously and indirectly by probing for job dislikes. If this fails, however, we have to approach the situation more directly with a softened follow-up question such as "How did you happen to leave that job?"

In posing this question, the interviewer should of course give particular attention to her own facial expressions and vocal intonations, in order to give the appearance of seeming as disarming and permissive as possible. Even so, some candidates may not give the real reason why they left a certain job. The interviewer must be alert for any indication of rationalization, since this type of response usually means the individual is trying to hide the real reason by attempting to explain away the situation. If an interviewer is not convinced that a person is telling the truth, she certainly should not challenge him at this point. To do so would be to risk loss of rapport and subsequent lack of spontaneous discussion throughout the remainder of the interview. Rather, she should wait until the interview is nearly concluded—when there is little or nothing to lose. If she is still interested in the candidate's qualifications, she can reintroduce the subject by asking him more directly to elaborate upon his reasons for the job change in question.

When a candidate leaves a number of jobs to make a little more money on subsequent ones, she may represent the kind of person who has too strong an economic drive. Strong desire to make money is a definite asset on some jobs—particularly those involving selling on a commission basis. The salesperson who wants to make a lot of money is usually one who will work harder to get it. At the same time, when the economic drive becomes too strong, the individual often becomes something of an opportunist, immediately jumping into any new situation that pays a little more. Such a person seldom develops strong loyalties, and the interviewer has a right to think, "Since this person has a habit of leaving each job whenever she gets a chance to make a little more money, I wonder how long we would be able to keep her happy here?"

When a candidate leaves a series of jobs because of dissatisfaction with job duties or working conditions, he may be the type of person who lacks perseverance and follow-through. Perhaps unable to take the bitter with the sweet, he "pulls up stakes" whenever he is confronted with anything really difficult or not to his liking. If such proves to be the case, a clear indication of immaturity will be apparent. When dissatisfaction appears to be chronic from job to job, the individual concerned may be poorly adjusted emotionally.

If discussion of a series of jobs indicates friction with supervisors or co-workers, interviewers should look specifically for indications of quick temper, inflexibility, intolerance, oversensitivity, and immaturity. When they suspect the possible existence of some of these traits, they should use such a question as "How did you feel about your relationships with your superiors and associates on that job? Were you completely satisfied with these relationships or, in retrospect, do you think they could have been improved to some extent?"

Discussion of reasons for leaving jobs may provide clues to assets as well as liabilities. In talking about a previous job from which he had been fired, for example, a candidate may assume some of the blame, indicating that he was "just off base" in that situation. Such candor often reflects objectivity, honesty, and maturity. In leaving certain job situations, moreover, the individual may demonstrate such positive factors as initiative and desire for further growth and development. If she has been in a dead-end situation with little opportunity for promotion, she certainly cannot be blamed for leaving it. If she is a person of considerable ability and leaves a given job to obtain broader experience and responsibility, this is again something that one should expect in any competent individual.

In discussing job changes, it is often helpful to explore how such changes came about. Did the candidate take the initiative herself? Did the suggestion come from her superiors? Or was she recruited for a better job by another company? The latter, incidentally, may tell something about her general reputation in her field.

A certain number of job changes over a period of some years is to be expected. Many people have good reasons for leaving one job to go to another—to increase their earnings, enhance their opportunities for promotion, and broaden their experience. In some occupations, such as advertising, rather frequent job change is considered standard. An advertising agency may obtain a large account and hire as many as 30 or 40 additional people to handle this additional business. At the end of the year, the agency may lose the account and be forced to terminate a considerable number of its employees.

Leadership Experience

Throughout the discussion of work experience, interviewers should carefully note the frequency with which candidates have been promoted to supervisory responsibility, together with their reactions to such responsibility. If individuals have derived considerable satisfaction from this kind of experience, and if they have been asked frequently to take over the direction of others, they are quite probably people of leadership ability. Certainly, a number of their previous superiors have thought so. Moreover, people who have led successfully in any situation have acquired skills in handling others that nothing but experience of this sort will provide.

In evaluating the possible effectiveness of an individual as a supervisor, look specifically for demonstrated ability to communicate, to plan and organize, to delegate important responsibilities to others, to be enthusiastic, to be fair, and to be sensitive to the feelings of others. It is equally important to find out whether the individual has shown a tendency to be autocratic or, in contrast, has been able to motivate other people to work because they like and respect him or her.

Discussing Work History with Experienced Candidates

Candidates 35 or older have such a body of work experience that very early experience becomes less meaningful and too time-consuming to explore. Instead of asking such candidates to discuss every single job they had while attending high school and college, interviewers should say, "Did you have any jobs during high school or college that you believe appreciably stimulated your early growth and development?" If the response is affirmative, take the time to discover how that experience influenced development. Then proceed immediately to the first post-college position with the question: "How did you go about getting your first job after college?"

Since the last 10 years of an older person's work history are normally the most likely to yield clues to current behavior, pass rather quickly over the early post-college jobs, concentrating primarily on how the person got the job, how long he stayed, the beginning and ending earnings, and why he left. In the subsequent, more important positions, of course, take the time to explore duties, likes, dislikes, performance appraisals, and levels of responsibility. Since many older candidates will have had management experience, probe here for management style: "How would you describe your management style?" Then: "Do you think of yourself as a tough manager, an easy one, or somewhere in between?" Such questions often supply clues to mental toughness, an extremely important requisite for effective management. With older candidates, it is also very important to check the more recent experience with the job description in order to determine the possible "fit." As pointed out earlier, some high-level candidates even negotiate the job description in order to bring it more in line with their own desires and expertise.

Achievements

Once interviewers have discussed the candidates' complete job history—from the first position to the most recent assignment—they should try to help individuals summarize achievements, in terms of abilities and personality traits that have been brought to light as a result of their experience on various jobs. This is done by formally introducing the technique of *self-evaluation* for the first time in the interview.

In order to accomplish this, use the question that appears in the Interview Guide: *"What did you learn about your strengths as a result of working on all of those jobs? Did you find, for example, that you worked harder than the average person, got along better with people, organized things better, gave more attention to detail—just what?"* It will be noted that the technique of self-evaluation is introduced by means of a laundry-list question. This is because most individuals will not have taken the time to analyze their strengths in terms of the abilities and personality traits interviewers are seeking to identify.

Helping Candidates Discuss Their Assets. Interviewers should ask individuals to discuss their assets candidly, pointing out that they should do this objectively without any feeling that they are bragging. Immediately after each asset has been presented, interviewers should reinforce the situation by giving candidates a verbal pat on the back. If an individual indicates that he is a hard worker, for example, and if the interviewer has already seen abundant evidence of this trait, she might say, "I'm sure you are a very hard worker, and that's a wonderful asset to have!" On the other hand, if she has a question about the individual's motivation, she will simply nod her head, ask the candidate to indicate some of his other assets, and resolve to reintroduce the subject of hard work later on when talking about the individual's shortcomings.

Some candidates may find it difficult to list their real assets. The interviewer should stimulate the discussion by pointing out one or two strengths he has already observed. Thus, he might say, "Well, I have observed that you seem to get along unusually well with people, and this of course is a tremendous asset in any job situation." After "priming the pump" with one or two such observations, the interviewer should pass the conversational ball back to the candidate, asking her to tell about some of her other strong points. If she seems to be unable to come up with any additional assets on her own, make use of the *calculated pause,* in this way giving her an opportunity to organize her thoughts. If, after 10 or 12 seconds, she is still unable to come up with anything, the interviewer should "take her off the hook" by introducing another asset he has observed during the interview or that has come to light as a result of discussing performance appraisals on various jobs. In some cases, a considerable amount of "pump-priming" may be necessary before the candidate begins to talk about some of her own strengths, but the interviewer should wait her out, using as much patience as possible.

The interviewer should not leave this important subject until he has developed a significant list of genuine assets, even if he has to interject a number of these himself. Once the candidate has been encouraged to think critically about her own strengths, she frequently warms to the task and generates a considerable amount of very useful information. It is extremely important that the interviewer help the candidate develop a sizable list of assets, since this paves the way for a subsequent discussion of shortcomings. One cannot expect a person to discuss shortcomings at length if the candidate is not certain the interviewer is well-acquainted with his or her strengths.

When the list of strengths becomes sizable, many candidates become quite anxious to reveal some shortcomings in order to give the appearance of objectivity. Moreover, in successfully developing a list of the candidate's achievements, the interviewer will have planted the seed of self-evaluation at this relatively early stage of the interview. As a consequence, the candidate may spontaneously volunteer further self-evaluative material during discussion of subsequent areas of the interview: education and present social adjustment. It is for this reason that the technique of self-evaluation is introduced at this point of the interview.

Development Needs

Having had an opportunity to discuss his or her strengths at some length, a candidate normally finds it relatively easy to talk about some of the areas that need further development. However, since this represents the first real confrontation in terms of asking specifically about shortcomings, appropriate rationale must be provided. This subject can be introduced by the question that appears in the Interview Guide: *"What clues did you get as to your development needs as a result of working on those jobs? You know, we all have some shortcomings, and the person who can recognize them can do something about them. Was there a need to acquire more self-confidence, more tact, more self-discipline, to become firmer with people—just what?"* This question and the one pertaining to achievement appearing in the Interview Guide should be committed to memory, verbatim.

Helping Candidates Discuss Their Shortcomings. In discussing a candidate's developmental needs, always use the word "improvement" rather than "weaknesses," "faults," or "liabilities." The latter three words carry the connotation that the trait may be so serious that very little can be done about it. The word "improvement" implies that the trait is just a little short of what it might desirably be and that the person may be able to improve upon it or eliminate it. Use the phrase "ways in which you can improve yourself." Thus, instead of saying, "What are some other shortcomings?" it is better to say, "What are some other ways in which you might improve yourself?"

Immediately after each opportunity for improvement has been presented, the interviewer should "play it down," in much the same way that any other piece of unfavorable information is played down throughout the interview. When an individual admits, for example, the need to develop more self-confidence, the interviewer might say, "Well, confidence is a trait that a lot of people need to develop further. I'm sure your self-confidence will improve with more experience."

When a person admits a shortcoming, such as lack of mental toughness, the interviewer should play this down by complimenting the individual for having recognized it and for facing up to it. The interviewer may say, "You deserve credit for being able to recognize this. And, because you have recognized it, you probably have already taken certain steps toward eliminating it."

When the candidate finds it difficult or seems reluctant to present any opportunities for improvement, the interviewer may stimulate the discussion by the use of *double-edged questions*. If an interviewer has already noted that the candidate is quite lacking in self-discipline, for example, she may say, "What about self-discipline? Do you think you have as much of this as you would like to have, or does this represent an area in which you could improve to some extent?" Such a question makes it easy for a person to admit shortcomings. Again, if the interviewer has noticed a general tendency to be lazy, she might say, "What about work habits? Do you think that you usually work as hard as you should, or is this something that you could improve a little bit?"

For the most part, indicated shortcomings can be taken pretty much at face value. Seldom will one draw attention to shortcomings that do not really exist. At the same time, there is the occasional individual—one who is exceedingly insecure and tends to underestimate his or her abilities—who will bring up something as a shortcoming that is not a deficiency.

The interviewer's role in the self-evaluation discussion is a pivotal one. If he tries to stimulate the discussion by introducing assets or shortcomings that are not part of the candidate's makeup, the latter quickly loses respect for him. On the other hand, if he is able to introduce traits that go to the very heart of the individual's personality and motivational pattern, the latter gains appreciable respect for him.

The Value of the Self-Evaluation Technique

As noted above, this technique can be of considerable value to both candidates and interviewers. Candidates gain by getting a clearer picture of their strengths and developmental needs, thus acquiring greater insight. Interviewers gain because they are frequently able to get more documentary evidence concerning a given candidate's overall qualifications.

When interviewers are able to get candidates to agree with them on the presence or absence of certain traits, this provides strong support for the original hypothesis. When, for example, an interviewer has seen several clues to insecurity throughout the interview, she waits expectantly for some indication of this in the candidate's self-evaluation. If lack of self-confidence is admitted spontaneously, or admitted as a result of probing with a double-edged question, the interviewer has of course developed further confirmation of her original hypothesis. And since the person is aware of this developmental need, he may be able to do something about improving himself in this respect.

Occasionally the candidate will mention a trait that may not have consciously crystallized in the interviewer's mind but for which he sees abundant evidence as soon as it is verbalized. He may have been only vaguely aware of the trait but, when the candidate mentions it specifically, he can immediately think of a number of clues that actually pointed in that direction. If the candidate had not mentioned this trait, the interviewer might not have factored it into his overall decision. When the candidate mentions an asset or shortcoming for which the interviewer has seen no support, it is well to ask the individual to elaborate. Subsequent remarks may convince the interviewer that the candidate actually possesses the trait in question, thus bringing to light valuable information that might otherwise have been missed.

In dealing with young candidates who have had limited work experience, do not confine the discussion of strengths and shortcomings to the work situation alone. Broaden the laundry-list question as follows: "What did you learn about your strengths as a result of working on those jobs or as a result of any other life experience?"

FACTORS OF JOB SATISFACTION

At this point, the interviewer has not only discussed the candidate's jobs, but has tried to plant the seed of self-evaluation by asking for a summary of strengths and developmental needs. We can now give our attention to another very fruitful area—factors of job satisfaction. This subject can be introduced with the laundry-list question on the Interview Guide: *"What does a job have to have to give you satisfaction? Some people look for money, some look for security, some want to manage, some want to create—what is important to you?"* Again, the candidate's response to such a depth question may provide clues to analytical ability and intellectual depth.

One individual may say, "Oh, I just want a job where I can be happy and make a good living." Another person may reflect a great deal more discernment and intellectual depth by such a remark as "In looking for a new job, I have given this subject a great deal of thought. I am looking primarily for an opportunity to grow and develop—to find the type of job that will provide the greatest challenge and do the most to bring out the best in me. Money is important, but I consider that secondary. Security probably ranks at the bottom of my list, since I feel that I can always make a living somewhere." A response such as this tells the interviewer a good bit about the individual's drives and aspirations, as well as about the quality of his or her thinking. The candidate's lack of emphasis on security, moreover, may provide a clue to his or her self-confidence.

If a candidate "blocks" at this point, give him a chance to organize his thinking by making use of the *calculated pause*. If he still seems to have a problem, repeat part of your laundry-list question or select one of the items and ask him rather directly how he feels about it. The interviewer may say, "Well, how do you feel about security, for example? Is this important to you or perhaps not?"

Discussion of job-satisfaction factors presents the interviewer with an excellent opportunity to obtain further confirmation of clues that have come to her attention earlier in the work discussion. For example, if she has noted some dislike for detail, she can include the phrase "Some like detail while others do not" in her laundry-list question. If the candidate seizes upon this with the statement, "Well, for one thing, I certainly do not want to be involved with such detail; I prefer to delegate this to others," the interviewer is presented with additional confirmation of her original hypothesis.

When candidates appear to have answered the question on job satisfaction to the best of their ability, probe further, using some of the items in parentheses at the end of this question in the Interview Guide. Say, for example, "What else should a job have to give you satisfaction? Should it be structured or unstructured?" Once that has been answered, say, "Should it be more theoretical or more practical?" After that response, say, "If you had a choice, would you prefer a job that had a fair amount of detail or one that did not have so much?" Responses to these questions can throw further light on factors that may enhance optimal placement. Factors of job satisfaction represent a very fruitful area for discussion: hence, at least four or five minutes should be devoted to this subject. The interviewer should then mentally compare the candidate's expressed desires with the specifications of the position in question.

Type of Job Desired

The work-history discussions should be concluded with a question concerning the kind of job the candidate is seeking. When a candidate says she really does not know what she wants, the interviewer should attempt to narrow the field for her. In the case of a recently graduated engineer, for example, he could say, "Well, do you think you might prefer basic research, development work, production, or technical service work?" The interviewer would then try to get the individual's reaction to these fields of work and compare these reactions with what he has already learned about the person as a result of the previous discussion. The individual frequently does a little self-evaluation at this point. She may say, "Well, I certainly know that I don't want research or development work. I learned in school that I am no whiz on a purely technical assignment."

If, on the basis of available test results and previous work-history discussion, the interviewer concurs with the candidate, he may then explore the individual's possible interest in production or technical service. Or he may decide to postpone this particular discussion until the end of the interview—until he has learned more about the individual and thus has a better basis for helping her with her placement decision.

As the work-history discussion draws to a close, the interviewer mentally reflects on the candidate's total job accomplishment. Has the individual made normal progress in terms of salary? Has he acquired a solid background of experience in his specialty? Has he shown an ability to assume gradually increased responsibility? If the answer to any of these important questions is negative, the interviewer may begin to have a real reservation concerning the candidate's overall qualifications. In some cases, the situation may be so clear-cut that the interviewer can decide then and there not to hire the candidate. In such a situation, she would talk very briefly about the individual's educational background and then terminate the discussion. Not only is it unfair to waste the candidate's time, but the interviewer also has to be economical with her time too.

EEO Considerations

1. Most members of minority groups need no special consideration with regard to the interpretation of work history. Their achievement speaks for itself.

2. There are other minority men and women whose work history does not appear very impressive because they have not yet been given an opportunity to demonstrate what they really can do. Since interviewers must try to *screen in* as many minorities as possible, it becomes their job to identify those individuals who have potential for greater achievement than their work history would seem to indicate. Some of the following areas may give evidence of such potential:

   a. Probe especially for how each job was obtained, as a possible indication of initiative.

   b. Look for any increased responsibility within a job, even though the job may have been rather routine. For example, the individual may have been promoted to lower levels of supervision such as crew leader, or chief clerk.

   c. Give special attention to indications of hard work, such as extremely long hours or physically demanding job duties. A good question here: "To what extent was that job physically demanding?"

3. Do not be critical of job changes when the new jobs represent increasingly better situations. We cannot expect a person to stay with a low-level, uninteresting job for any great length of time if advancement is possible elsewhere. In probing for reasons for changing jobs, then, try to determine whether or not the new job really did represent a measurable improvement over the previous one or whether the hopping from job to job is because the person finds it difficult to stay put.

In discussing factors of job satisfaction, give favorable consideration to the man or woman who seems to have a genuine desire to make something better of himself or herself, even though the individual may not yet have been given much of an opportunity. People who have not given up hope deserve more consideration than those who have become cynical or pessimistic.

With all candidates, the discussion of strengths and shortcomings at the end of the work history will be difficult. Interviewers must therefore exercise great patience in developing this information. They may have to do more "pump-priming" in terms of introducing strengths and shortcomings that they have observed during the interview. But, once candidates have acquired a definite understanding of what they are expected to do, they can often come up with very valuable information about themselves.

Chapter Twelve
Interpreting Education and Ability to Work on a Team

Candidates for most higher-level jobs will usually be college graduates, and many will have gone to graduate school. These years represent a large segment of the individual's life, during which time he or she has had ample opportunity to develop a considerable number of assets or shortcomings. Interpretation of the educational history, then, is not only concerned with whether or not the individual has acquired sufficient training to carry out the job in question; it is also concerned with the evaluation of abilities, personality traits, and motivation gained during the experience.

In the case of younger candidates, the educational experience may represent the most important period of the individual's life so far and, as such, may provide the greatest source of clues to behavior. Although education does not represent quite such a dominant factor in the case of older candidates, it is nevertheless exceedingly important. The traits individuals develop while in school often remain with them throughout life. Moreover, the discussion of educational history frequently provides additional confirming evidence of traits that had been tentatively identified during the discussion of work experience.

STRUCTURING THE DISCUSSION OF EDUCATION

Having completed the discussion of work history, the interviewer uses a comprehensive introductory question to launch the subject of education. In so doing, he tries to make the transition from the first interview area to the second in such a way that the discussion appears to be a continuing conversation, rather than a segmented one.

The interviewer may preface his comprehensive introductory question by saying, "That gives me a very good picture of your work experience; now tell me something about your education and training." In the comprehensive introductory question, the interviewer should point out that he would like to have the candidate talk about such factors as subject preferences, grades, and extracurricular activities.

In response to a comprehensive introductory question, the candidate will normally discuss much of her school experiences spontaneously. If she leaves out important items or does not discuss certain topics in sufficient detail, the interviewer will use appropriate follow-up questions to get the complete story. He will also use such questions to probe more deeply for the underlying implication of certain of the candidate's remarks. After the individual completes the discussion of her college experience, he may wish to repeat part of his comprehensive introductory question by saying, "Suppose you tell me a little more about high school [or college] now—your subject preferences, grades, extracurricular activities, and the like."

Grades

If the candidate does not specifically mention grades, the interviewer may say, "What about grades? Were they average, above average, or perhaps a little below average?" Note that such a question makes it easier for the individual to admit grades that were below average. If grades were above average, an attempt should be made to determine the candidate's actual ranking in the class. Was it upper half, upper third, upper quarter, or upper tenth? When a person provides a ranking, such as ninth in the class, he or she should be asked about the number in the class. A standing of ninth in a class of 400, for example, would represent a real achievement, but ninth in a class of 50 would be a lot less impressive.

College Boards

The majority of college graduates today will have taken SATs (Scholastic Aptitude Tests) during their senior year of high school, and most of these people will have been told their specific scores. Scores on these tests give us a good "fix" on the candidate's mental ability, verbal ability, and quantitative or numerical ability. People under the age of 25 or 26 are likely to remember their scores.

High school seniors take two specific tests prepared by the Educational Testing Service in Princeton, New Jersey—one test on verbal ability and another test on quantitative or numerical ability. A perfect score on each of these two tests is 800. The table below represents the distribution of scores on each of the two tests by the high school senior population.

Test Score	Interpretation
700-800	Excellent
575-700	Above average
425-575	Average
300-425	Below average
Below 300	Poor

Today, the colleges with the highest academic standards look for a combined score on these two tests of 1300 to 1350. This means that a student might be taken into a good engineering school with a verbal score of 575 and a numerical score of 725, since the engineering course content places greater demand on mathematical aptitude. Or, one with a score of 750 on verbal ability might be accepted into a top school of journalism even though her math score was no more than 550.

Even the less prestigious schools look for a minimum combined score on the SATs of at least 1000. Hence, a score of less than 500 on either the verbal or the math test reflects a relatively low aptitude for a person who has graduated from college. And, of course, the higher the score, the better the aptitude.

Although most young people will have been told their college board scores and will remember them because of their importance in getting into the college of their choice, some may be reluctant to disclose their scores, particularly if they are not especially good. As a result, they may simply say they have forgotten the scores. Failure to reveal SAT scores should not be regarded as a clue to dishonesty. An individual has a right to withhold this information.

In approaching this question, the interviewer *assumes consent* with such a direct question as "What were your college board scores?" Note that she does not say, "Do you remember your college board scores?" or "Did you take the college board examinations?" Candidates are much more likely to respond to a direct, definitive question here since the interviewer does not make it easy for them to "get off the hook." If they profess not to remember their scores, the interviewer can say, "Well, were they in the 500s, 600s, or 700s?" Or she may say, "Did you do better on the verbal or the mathematical test?"

Most younger people will respond to the question on college board scores, particularly if good rapport has been established and maintained. The resulting information—providing you feel that you can believe the individual—can be unusually helpful, particularly if it is consistent with clues to intelligence and aptitudes that have come to light previously. Of course, since some candidates may not remember their SAT scores correctly or may even lie about them, if the reported scores do not seem consistent with other clues to aptitudes they should be disregarded.

The tests are normally taken in the junior year of high school for practice and then again in the senior year. The latter represents the official score and is often appreciably better than the score achieved during the junior year. Hence, the interviewer must make certain that the scores the person provides resulted from tests taken during the senior year.

Extracurricular Activities

The degree to which individuals have participated in extracurricular activities may provide many important clues to personality traits. If little or no participation has taken place, individuals may have a tendency to be shy, self-conscious, inhibited, and introverted. In fact, they may freely admit that they tended to be "backward" and retiring at that stage of their lives. Of course, such people may have changed materially over the years, but the chances are very good that certain vestiges of these shortcomings may remain today. On the other hand, people may say that they did not participate in student activities because they did not care very much for their classmates. Such a remark should prompt the interviewer to determine if this is an indication of snobbishness, intolerance, or a "sour grapes" attitude.

Effort

The amount of effort expended in order to get good grades—a topic almost completely disregarded by most untrained interviewers—can often provide one of the most important keys to the assessment of intellect and motivation. If a candidate obtained good grades in a school with high academic standards without working very hard, possession of good mental ability can be assumed. On the other hand, if no better-than-average grades were obtained in a school with questionable academic standards despite unusual effort, there would seem to be some question about the level of mental ability. The latter individual, however, can be given credit for strong motivation. It is not unusual for such a person to say, "I really had to work for everything I got. I certainly burned a lot of midnight oil. In fact, I used to be envious of my roommate who was always able to get things twice as easily as I could."

When interpreting grades in terms of the amount of effort expended, it is also necessary to factor in the amount of time spent on extracurricular activities as well as time spent on part-time jobs. People with average grades in a good school who have devoted a great deal of time to student activities or to financing their own education deserve credit for their overall accomplishments. Such people often develop social skills and work habits that stand them in good stead later in life. Moreover, people who crowd in a great many activities, do a considerable amount of part-time work, and also manage to make good grades are usually the kind of people who have learned to organize their time effectively. Normally, they work on a specific schedule and do a considerable amount of planning.

Special Achievements

Interviewers should be alert to the possibility that certain individuals may have attained achievements beyond those of most of their class-mates, and such achievements may provide additional clues to mental ability, specific aptitudes, and leadership strength. Some individuals are basically modest and may not reveal this type of information unless they are specifically asked to do so. For instance, a liberal arts student may indicate that she had "good" grades in college, while not indicat-ing she was Phi Beta Kappa. People achieving such honors are normal-ly those who possess both high mental ability and strong motivation.

Participation in college sports can also provide personality clues. It is good to ask an athlete if she was ever elected captain of a team. Again, responsibility of this kind fosters the development of leadership traits. In the case of persons elected to student government or to stu-dent body president, the interviewer has a right to assume that such individuals were popular with their contemporaries and probably pos-sessed some degree of leadership ability. Of course, school politics is responsible for the fact that some people are elected to class offices, but the people involved usually display some traits that set them apart from the crowd. At the very least, they are ordinarily liked by others, have a genuine interest in people, and have developed an ability to get along amicably with people on all levels.

Graduate-Level Training

Interviewers explore this area immediately after getting the complete description of the college experience. Even in the case of those who do not have graduate training it is good to ask, "Did you ever think about going to graduate school?" A question such as this frequently provides clues to the strength of the individual's theoretical drive.

Interviewers explore graduate training in much the same way that they carried out the college discussion, concentrating on subject pref-erences, grades, amount of effort involved, and any special achieve-ments. In some graduate schools, grades are either satisfactory or un-satisfactory, but other schools give letter grades, insisting that courses counted for graduate credit must be at a B level or better. In such a case, it is interesting to learn whether the graduate student obtained mostly B's and a few A's or made practically a straight-A record.

Special attention should be devoted to the individual's thesis or dissertation. Even though the candidate's field may not be very familiar to the interviewer, the latter can still ask about the problems she encountered and how she went about solving such problems. Evidence of creative ability may be revealed here, particularly in cases where the candidate solved most of her own problems rather than relying upon her sponsors. It is also good to ask about the extent to which the research findings may be expected to make a contribution to the field. In some cases, individuals publish articles in technical journals even before they are awarded their degrees. In evaluating graduate training, again consider the academic standards of the school. A Ph.D. from some schools means a great deal more than it does from others.

Consideration of postgraduate training, though, should not be confined to formal courses taken with a view to getting a master's or doctoral degree. Many people take special courses of one kind or another, including extension work, correspondence courses, and company-sponsored courses. Moreover, many such courses are taken at night, after putting in a full day on the job. Such attempts to improve oneself frequently provide clues to perseverance, aspiration, and energy level. In going to school at night, individuals often extend their capacity for constructive effort. Many courses taken in the evening also equip people to turn in a better performance on their jobs.

How Was Education Financed?

The interviewer will have acquired much of this information as a result of having discussed the candidate's early jobs under work history. But it is good to reconsider such information mentally while discussing the candidate's educational background. As already indicated, awareness of the fact that candidates worked their way through school may cast a different light on the kind of grades they received or on the extent of their participation in extracurricular activities. Individuals who have to work their way through school with part-time jobs frequently develop greater maturity and motivation than people who did not have to earn any of their college expenses. When individuals help finance their own education, they usually appreciate it all the more and try to get the most out of it. In the course of this experience, they frequently develop sound work habits, perseverance, and resourcefulness.

In contrast, people whose parents pay for their entire education may become accustomed to having things too easy. In fact, they may suffer a rude shock when they do finally get out into the world and find it necessary to earn their own living. Certainly in those cases adjustment to industry will be more difficult than for people who have already learned to earn their own way.

Many people will say that if they had it to do over again they would borrow money rather than work so hard while going to college. They seem to feel that they missed a great deal by not being able to participate in extracurricular activities, for example. All things considered, the greatest overall development probably comes to the student who tries to maintain some kind of balance with respect to academic work, extracurricular activities, and part-time jobs. Too much concentration on any one of the three at the expense of the others usually has some retarding effect on the overall growth of the individual.

When the interviewer concludes the discussion of education, the entire experience is mentally evaluated in terms of the extent to which it has equipped the person to handle the job under consideration. In making this evaluation, formal courses in high school and college, training acquired while in military service, special company-sponsored courses, extension work, and correspondence courses are all included. Then the interviewer considers whether or not the candidate has the specialized training that the job requires, whether the candidate has developed the necessary skills, and, equally important, whether or not the candidate has developed the kind of thinking demanded for the job in question. Many job descriptions indicate simply that the incumbent should be a college graduate, and this is not enough.

Obviously, too, the interviewer will evaluate the educational history in terms of clues to abilities, personality traits, and motivation. Particular interest should be paid to those clues that supply further confirming evidence to support interpretive hypotheses established in the discussion of the candidate's work experience. It is to be expected that the interviewer will have picked up some new clues to behavior that did not come to light during the earlier discussion.

WELL-ROUNDEDNESS

After completing the discussion of the candidates' education, interviewers begin to explore social adjustment. As will be noted below, outside interests and hobbies often help determine the extent to which candidates are reasonably well-adjusted socially. As in the case of all the other interview areas, this discussion can also provide many clues to other traits and abilities. In particular, the resulting information often brings into focus such factors as sociability and intellectual breadth and depth. Obviously, discussion in this area is usually less significant in the case of young men and women just out of college than with somewhat older individuals. In talking with young people about their extracurricular activities in college, interviewers will already have learned a great deal about their social adjustment.

Interviewers lead candidates into this area by means of a simple question concerning interests and hobbies. Such a question as "Well, now, what are some of the things that you like to do for fun and recreation outside of work?" will usually launch this discussion very effectively. And much of the information developed in this area may provide confirming evidence of clues to behavior developed earlier in the interview.

Community Involvement

Community involvement also offers an opportunity for practice in social situations. Activities associated with a church, local government, or various community clubs not only provide practice in getting along with people, but may very well offer opportunities for leadership. Such activities, moreover, often reflect the type of person who takes their community responsibilities seriously and cares enough to get involved. More often than not, such people reflect the attributes of solid citizens and tend to be people of good character.

Energy Level

High energy level, vigor, and stamina obviously are extremely important assets. In fact, few people attain genuine career achievement unless they possess these important qualities in some abundance. Given a reasonable degree of intellect, educational training, and personality effectiveness, the degree of energy and stamina a person possesses may account in large part for his or her ability to win promotions over associates.

By the time interviewers have reached this stage of the discussion, they will have acquired numerous clues to individuals' energy level and stamina. If interviewers are not certain of a candidate's amount of energy at this stage of an interview, they may ask about this by saying, "How would you describe your energy level—as average, somewhat above average, or perhaps a little below average?"

Outside Interests and Social Adjustment

Just as interviewers mentally review other areas of the interview upon completing them, so should they try to determine what the discussion of outside interests has told them about a given individual's social adjustment. Do interests reflect a "loner" who seems to have no friends and is not an altogether cheerful or happy individual? Such findings may provide clues to lack of emotional adjustment. This shortcoming may also be reflected in people who "bite off more than they can chew" and who spread themselves so thin that they find it difficult to marshal all their energies and focus them appropriately on a given task.

People with good social adjustment are normally those who enjoy the companionship of others, who participate in enough activities so their lives are relatively full, and who are capable of deriving genuine satisfaction from achievements.

Chapter Thirteen | Terminating the Interview and Completing the Interview Rating Form

With the completion of the third part of the Interview Guide, interviewers are ready to terminate the interview and subsequently to write the interview report. Under optimal conditions, the report of interview findings should be written immediately after completion of the interview. With interview data fresh in mind, interviewers should be able to write the report in a fraction of the time it would take should they wait several hours after finishing the interview.

TERMINATING THE INTERVIEW

As noted earlier, it is occasionally permissible to terminate an interview before all the suggested background areas have been discussed. This is only done in cases where a predominance of negative information results from the early discussion. If, after a discussion of the work history, for example, it becomes clearly evident that the candidate is not at all suited for the job in question, the interview may be terminated at that point.

However, the interviewer should guard against snap judgments, making certain that the decision not to carry the interview any further is

149

based upon adequate factual evidence rather than an emotional reaction to the individual concerned. There are occasions, too, when interviewers' impressions of a candidate may change materially after the first half hour of discussion, swinging from a rather negative impression to an entirely positive one. The accumulation of negative findings must be substantial to justify an early interview termination.

Termination, in the sense that we are using it here, involves more than the windup of the information-*gathering* aspects of the interview. It also includes the information-*giving* aspects. Every candidate should be given some information about the company and about the job for which he or she is being considered.

TERMINATING THE UNQUALIFIED CANDIDATE

Even in the case where the candidate is to be rejected, a certain amount of information-giving should take place at the end of the interview. Directed toward the objective of public relations, this should be kept general. In other words, the candidate should be told about general factors such as company organization, company policy, products manufactured, and the like—rather than about specific factors such as wages, hours of work, and employee benefits. The latter are important only in the case of a candidate who is to be offered a position. Five minutes will ordinarily prove sufficient to tell the unqualified candidate about the company. However, courteous and informative answers should always be given to any questions raised.

Terminate the interview on a positive tone. A statement such as the following will often accomplish this objective: "Well, you certainly have a long list of impressive assets—assets that will stand you in good stead throughout your working life. And, at the same time, you seem to have some insight into the areas to which you should give your attention in terms of further development. I will discuss your qualifications with other interested persons within the company and will let you know the outcome within a day or two. Thank you very much for coming in; I certainly enjoyed talking with you."

Once the interviewer has decided to terminate the discussion, this should be done with dispatch. Otherwise, the conversation will deteriorate into meaningless chitchat. After this kind of concluding statement, the interviewer should stand up, shake hands, and escort the candidate to the door.

Rejection of candidates is always a difficult task at best and must be handled with care and finesse. First and foremost, candidates must be rejected in such a way that their feelings are not unduly hurt and their self-confidence is not undermined. In the second place, the company's public relations are at stake. In other words, rejected candidates should be permitted to "save face," so that they do not bear ill will toward the company.

Because this task requires so much skill and finesse, many companies prefer to inform candidates of an unfavorable employment decision by letter. Actually, the latter means is almost uniformly used in the case of candidates for high-level jobs. A carefully worded letter not only represents an expression of courtesy but carries the implication of more thorough consideration. Nevertheless, the letter should be sent within a day or two after the interview, thus freeing the unsuccessful candidate to concentrate on other job possibilities.

The reason for the rejection should be phrased in terms of the job demands rather than in terms of the individual's personal qualifications. The candidate should be given credit for his or her real assets but, at the same time, should be told that, in the interviewer's opinion, the job will not make the best use of the candidate's abilities. This approach simply implies that he or she will probably be better suited in some other job with another company.

TERMINATING THE INTERVIEW OF THE QUALIFIED CANDIDATE

Although the interviewer ordinarily has the authority to reject unqualified candidates, final responsibility for placing qualified candidates on the payroll usually rests with the line manager to which the candidate is being referred. Even when the interviewer's decision is entirely favorable, this should not be communicated to the candidate. Rather, the interviewer should express real interest in the individual's qualifications, assuring the candidate that the line manager will schedule a later meeting.

The information-giving aspect of the interview takes on even greater importance when the interviewer's decision is favorable. In these situations, everything possible is done to sell the candidate on the job. And the interviewer is in a unique position to do this. With the full knowledge of the candidate's abilities and qualifications in mind, the extent to which these qualifications apply to the job can be specifically pointed out. Where the decision is favorable, moreover, the interviewer should talk in terms of job specifics—earnings, employee benefits, and subsequent opportunities for promotion. Company policies, products, and the organization's position in the industry can be explained. At the same time, the interviewer will be careful not to oversell the job, knowing that this might lead to eventual disappointment and poor morale.

COMPLETING THE INTERVIEW RATING FORM

The write-up of the case represents an important, integral part of the interviewing process. As the results are recorded, the interviewer's thinking crystallizes with respect to the candidate's qualifications. By the time the candidate leaves the room, the interviewer will normally have decided whether the person is qualified for the job in question. But the write-up of the case represents an extension of this decision-making.

In the process of recording the findings, the interviewer isolates out value judgments and is normally able to assign a more precise rating to the candidate's qualifications. The case report forces interviewers to weigh all the relevant factors; as a consequence they are usually in a much better position to decide whether the candidate's qualifications merit a slightly above-average rating, a well-above-average rating, or perhaps an excellent rating.

Because the recording of interview findings represents such an essential aspect of the entire process, the Interview Rating Form should be completed immediately after the candidate leaves the room.

With all the essential facts still fresh in mind, the interviewer usually finds it possible to complete the form within 45 minutes. If this task is postponed, twice the amount of time may be required, and even then all the salient information may not be recalled.

In writing on the Interview Rating Form, use the space provided under each interview area for recording major findings pertinent to that area. Since the space is obviously limited, the interviewer will have to decide which findings in each area contribute most to understanding the candidate's behavior and overall qualifications for the job in question. The recording of interview results should not be confined to facts alone, since many of these facts will already have appeared on the application blank. Rather, the interviewers should try to indicate their interpretation of these facts, in terms of the extent to which they may provide clues to the individual's personality, motivation, or character.

PERSONALITY AND ABILITY

In the chapters on interpretation, we noted that interviewers with proper training and practice will normally know whether or not they wish to hire a candidate by the time that individual leaves the room. This is because they have been picking up clues to behavior throughout the discussion of work history, education, and outside interests. By the end of the interview, they have acquired sufficient hard, factual documentation to support an objective employment decision. Even so, reference to the personality and ability configurations detailed in Figure 13-1 should enable an interviewer to become more definitive with respect to the individual's make-up.

Reference to the personality and ability configurations also helps interviewers make a relatively quick assessment of a candidate's strengths and shortcomings. Some interviewers find it helpful, moreover, to use these configurations to complete the summary of assets and shortcomings of the Interview Rating Form immediately following the completion of the interview. Once having completed this summary, they work backward in a sense, making certain that their write-up of work experience, education, and present social adjustment contains abundant documentation of the assets and shortcomings they have already summarized.

Writing the Work History

Data should be recorded chronologically, in much the same way as it is obtained during the interview. Thus, there should be a brief treatment of early jobs, followed by a discussion of post-college jobs in chronological order. Because of space limitations, early jobs may be treated as a group rather than discussed singly. The discussion should be primarily interpretive, drawing upon factual information to highlight clues to personality, motivation, and character. Obviously, it is impossible to draw off meaningful interpretations from every single fact presented, but clues to behavior should nevertheless be sprinkled frequently throughout the discussion of work history.

At the end of the work history discussion, the interviewer should be sure to indicate an evaluation of the candidate's work experience and its relevance in terms of the job under consideration. Figure 13-1 represents a template of how work experience should be recorded on the Interview Rating Form.

Primary		
Mental Ability	**Motivation**	**Maturity**
verbal aptitude	energy	judgment
math aptitude	willingness to work	knowledge of self
analytical power	conscientiousness	reasonable vocational
perceptiveness	initiative	goals
critical thinking	self-discipline	lack of tendency to
intellectual breadth	perseverance	rationalize
and depth	aspirations	awareness of
	personal standards	limitations
		ability to "take the
		bitter with the
		sweet"

Figure 13-1. Interview rating categories for the Interview Rating Form (continued on next page)

Secondary		
People Skills	**Technical Ability**	**Leadership**
tact	math aptitude	assertiveness
empathy	academic preparation	self-confidence
sensitivity to the needs	analytical ability	tough mindedness
of others	critical thinking	good communication
friendliness	creativity	skills
cooperativeness	attention to detail	enthusiasm
		organization
		boldness in thinking
		a take-charge person
Character	**Emotional Adjustment**	**Aptitude for Manufacturing**
honesty	ability to take pressure	sense of urgency
reliability	cheerful outlook on	production mindedness
good value system	life	motivation to get the
	not a worrier	pieces out of the
	not subject to wide	door
	mood swings	flexibility
		strong leadership
		ability to keep several
		balls in the air
		simultaneously
		tough-mindedness
Aptitude for Sales		**Aptitude for Finance**
assertiveness		math aptitude
self-confidence		academic preparation
tough-mindedness		attention to detail
gift of gab		some introversion
infectious enthusiasm		ability to take a certain amount of
sense of humor		"number crunching"
perseverance		ability to see the big picture
charisma		
extroversion		

Figure 13-1. Continued

RATING EDUCATION AND TRAINING

As in the case of the treatment of the work history, educational data should also be recorded in chronological order. This means that initially there should be a discussion of the college experience, including any post-graduate work. Again, the recorded information should be largely interpretive, with a liberal use of factual data for documentation. Thus, actual grades and class standings should be noted here. Be sure to record extracurricular activities as well as the extent to which the individual seems to have applied himself or herself.

Here, as in the previous area, be sure to indicate names of schools, employers, and the like. This report should be sufficiently complete so the reader does not have to refer to the application blank for additional information. An example of the manner in which the educational information should be recorded appears below:

> Did exceptionally well in high school, graduating third in a class of 458 and doing her best work in math and science. College boards were 630 verbal (good) and 745 math (exceptional). Because she was very shy, Mary did not take part in extracurricular activities and did not date.

> Studied very hard at Swarthmore—a top school—and made outstanding grades (3.7 out of a possible 4.0), winning election to Tau Beta Pi during her junior year and graduating magna cum laude. Mary majored in electrical engineering and enjoyed all of the more theoretically oriented courses such as thermodynamics, circuitry, and higher math—a strong clue to her ability to think in the abstract. Also enjoyed and did well in her design courses. Began to "blossom out a bit" in college, becoming more socially engaged. Mary made an exceptional record at a top school and hence is unusually well trained academically. Obviously, too, she has superior intelligence both with respect to quantity and quality (analytical, perceptive, and critical ability).

Rating Well-Roundedness

Interpretive comments in this area should be concerned primarily with value judgments as to the person's interests and overall social adjustment. An illustration of such comments appears below:

Interests fairly broad and somewhat intellectual—reads five or six books a month, likes to make her own clothes, has student license as a pilot, and enjoys listening to classical music.

Energy level is admittedly no better than average and, in truth, may be somewhat less than average.

Pursues many of her activities by herself or, at best, with one or two other people. Admits that she does not have as much social facility as she would like.

Seems something of a "loner" and not altogether happy, raising a question concerning her emotional adjustment.

Rating Personality, Character, and Motivation

Each of the traits listed under this area is preceded by a set of parentheses. This permits the interviewer to assign a rating to each trait. As in the case of ratings made in all the other interview areas, value judgments should be formulated in terms of the demands of the job for which a person is being considered.

Using a five-point scale, the interviewer places a 5 in the parentheses to indicate the belief that the candidate has a high degree of the trait in question, a 4 if the individual is judged to have an above-average amount of the trait, a 3 if the candidate is judged to have an "average" or adequate amount of the trait, a 2 if the candidate is thought to have a below-average degree of the trait, and a 1 if the individual is evaluated to be seriously lacking in that characteristic. If the interviewer is unable to decide about a given trait or if the particular trait has no relevance in terms of the job under consideration, the parentheses are left blank.

In devising forms such as the Interview Rating Form, it is of course impossible to include all the traits of personality, motivation, and character that should be considered in evaluating candidate characteristics for a wide range of jobs. The characteristics listed on this particular form simply represent some of the traits that experience has shown to be most relevant in assessing candidates for high-level jobs in general. Other characteristics deemed of particular importance in a given case can be listed as representing either a strength or a shortcoming on Section V of the Interview Rating Form, the summary of assets and shortcomings.

The material presented below is designed to aid the interviewer in thinking through the various kinds of information that might be used to support a rating on each of the 14 traits listed on the back of the Interview Guide. The questions appearing below under each trait are designed simply to stimulate the interviewer's thinking, in terms of the kind of positive and negative information that would ordinarily be factored into the rating of that trait. Items preceded by a minus sign represent examples of unfavorable findings with respect to a given trait; those preceded by a plus sign represent examples of favorable or positive findings.

Maturity
+ Has she learned to accept her limitations and live with them?
+ Does she have well-formulated vocational goals?
+ Did she work during college summers to help pay tuition, even if parents could have afforded to pay the total amount?
+ Is there a responsible attitude toward her family?
− Is there any tendency to rationalize failures?
− Is there chronic dissatisfaction with job duties and working conditions, reflecting an inability to take the bitter with the sweet?
− Was effort in school confined only to those studies he liked?
− Does he rationalize academic failures by blaming the school or the teachers?

Emotional Adjustment
+ Has she shown an ability to maintain composure in the face of frustration?
+ Has he been able to maintain his emotional balance and mental health in the face of trying personal circumstances, such as a protracted period of unemployment?

+ Is she able to deal with the shortcomings of subordinates calmly and patiently?
+ Is there considerable evidence that she does not allow her emotions to color her judgment?
– Have there been problems with supervisors, teachers, or parents, which reflected a tendency to "fly off the handle"?
– Is he admittedly moody and inclined to experience more than the normal degree of ups and downs?
– Is she inclined to sulk in the face of criticism?
– Do current difficulties with peers seem to stem in part from a tendency to be sarcastic or hotheaded?

Teamworker

+ Does he seem to have operated successfully as a member of a team, in connection with sports activities in school, community activities in the neighborhood, or group activities on the job?
+ Does she seem to place the accomplishments of the group ahead of her personal feelings and ambitions?
+ Does he have the degree of tact and social sensitivity necessary for the establishment and maintenance of good interpersonal relations with other members of a team?
– Is he strongly motivated to be the "star" of the team, taking more than his share of credit for accomplishments?
– Did she have difficulty getting along with her associates while in the army or navy?
– Does she show any pronounced tendency to be inflexible, intolerant, or opinionated?

Sensitivity

+ Does the manner in which he phrased his remarks during the interview reflect tact and consideration for the interviewer?
+ In discussing her relationships with subordinates, does she seem to have reflected genuine consideration for their feelings?
+ Is he sensitive to the reactions of others to the extent that he is able to structure his approach without antagonizing them?
+ Does she show evidence of being a good listener?

– Has she talked disparagingly about minority groups?
– Has he made a number of remarks during the interview that have been unduly blunt and direct?

Adaptability

+ Has she shown a liking for jobs involving contact with many types of people and diverse situations?
+ Has he shown an ability to handle a number of job assignments simultaneously?
+ Has she demonstrated the ability to move from one job to a completely different kind of job without undue difficulty?
– Was he unable to do well in certain subjects "because of the teacher"?
– Was she raised in a provincial small town atmosphere where there was relatively limited exposure to diverse situations and different types of people?
– Does his approach to a job reflect such a tendency to be a perfectionist that he has to do everything "just so"?

Tough-Mindedness

+ Is he willing to take a stand for what he thinks is right?
+ Has she demonstrated an ability to make decisions involving people that, of necessity, work to the disadvantage of the few but have to be made for the good of the many?
+ Is she willing to delegate responsibilities even though inadequate performance on the tasks delegated may reflect directly upon her?
– Does she have a strong dislike for disciplining subordinates?
– Is he insufficiently demanding of subordinates, in the sense that he is reluctant to ask them to work overtime or to "push" them to some extent when there is a job to be done within a certain deadline?
– Is she a product of a soft, sheltered early work experience where there was little opportunity to become conditioned to the seamier side of existence?
– Does he give the impression of being too sympathetic or overly concerned about the feelings of others?

Self-Discipline

+ In connection with her academic career, has she shown a willingness to apply herself diligently to even those courses she disliked?

+ Does she assume her share of civic responsibility, even though community activities in general do not appeal to her?

+ Has she demonstrated a willingness to give first attention to those important aspects of a job that may be of less interest to her?

− Has he shown a tendency to procrastinate unduly in carrying out the less pleasant jobs assigned him?

− Did he fail to take full advantage of academic opportunities because he was not able to make himself "dig deeply enough" to really understand the subject?

− Has he been so conditioned by a soft, easy life that there has been relatively little need to cope with difficult problems or situations?

Initiative

+ Has he demonstrated an ability to operate successfully without close supervision?

+ Does he reach out for ever-increasing responsibility?

+ Is there any evidence to indicate that she is a self-starter, in the sense that she does not have to wait to be told what to do?

+ Has she demonstrated a willingness to depart from the status quo in order to accomplish a given task in a new and perhaps more efficient manner?

− Does she show a dislike for situations that have not been structured for her?

− Does he seem to have fallen into a job rut, in the sense that he has been unwilling to extricate himself from a dead-end situation?

Perseverance

+ Did he show perseverance in college by completing his undergraduate work despite a lack of good scholastic aptitude?

+ Once he starts a job, does he continue with it until it has been completed, resisting any tendency to become distracted?

+ Has she completed an appreciable portion of her college education by going to school at night?

- Has she changed jobs too frequently?
- Does he find it difficult to complete tasks on his own, such as correspondence courses where he does not have the stimulation of
  group effort?
- Is there evidence to support the view that she starts more things than
  she can finish?

Self-Confidence

+ Does he reflect a realistic appraisal of his abilities and a willingness
  to take action?
+ Does his general manner reflect poise and presence?
+ Does she have sufficient confidence in her assets so that she is willing to discuss her shortcomings objectively?
- Was confidence undermined by an overly demanding supervisor
  who tended to be a perfectionist?
- During the early years was she unable to compete successfully with
  those of her own age in athletics or in academics?
- Has he been reluctant to take on additional job responsibility because of fear of failure?
- Did she limit her extracurricular activities in school because she
  feared lack of acceptance by her classmates?

Assertiveness

+ Does his personality have considerable impact?
+ Has she participated in contact sports where aggressiveness represented an important requisite?
+ Has she operated successfully in sales, expediting, or production
  supervision—types of jobs conducive to the development of personal forcefulness?
+ Is his history replete with evidences of leadership in school, on the
  job, or in connection with activities in the community?
- Has he shown a tendency to let others take advantage of him because he lacks self-assertiveness?
- Does she tend to be introverted in the sense that she shies away from
  group activity?

Conscientiousness

+ Is he inclined upon occasion to work evenings and weekends, even though this is not actually required by his supervisor?
+ Does she have high personal standards for her work?
− Does her record on the job reflect a tendency to let things slide?
− Does he tend to be a clock-watcher?

Hard Worker

+ Has her history been such that she has become conditioned to hard work and long hours?
+ Did he get good grades in school despite limited mental ability?
+ Did she earn a relatively high percentage of her college expenses?
+ Has he had any experiences that may have extended his capacity for constructive effort, such as going to school at night while carrying on a full-time job during the day?
+ Does he seem to be in excellent health, reflecting a considerable amount of vigor and stamina?
− Does his general manner seem phlegmatic, reflecting a possible below-average energy level?
− Has she shown a strong dislike of overtime work?
− Does she seem always to look for the easy way out?

Honesty and Sincerity

+ Has she "come clean" during the interview discussion, in the sense that she has shown a willingness to talk about the unfavorable aspects of her background as well as the favorable aspects?
+ Is she willing to give credit where credit is due?
− Is there any evidence to support the view that he is exclusively oriented in the direction of personal gain, to the point that he does not develop strong loyalties to any organization or perhaps even to his own family?
− Does he seem to derive satisfaction from the discussion of situations where he has been able to get the better of the other fellow or to "pull a fast one"?
− Does she have any tendency to exaggerate her own accomplishments?

— Does his story seem to be inconsistent in terms of other selection findings, such as information developed from the application form, the preliminary interview, the aptitude tests, or the reference checkups?

WRITING THE SUMMARY OF ASSETS AND SHORTCOMINGS

Items listed under "Assets and Shortcomings" in this section of the Interview Rating Form should be concerned with the most important findings, in terms of the candidate's overall qualifications. And these items, for the most part, should represent a summation of a number of individual factors. For example, the interviewer would list as an asset an item such as "effective sales personality," rather than trying to list all the factors of which the so-called "sales personality" is composed, such as aggressiveness, sense of humor, poise, presence, social sensitivity, and persuasiveness.

The summary of assets and shortcomings should include major findings from all the selection steps, with special emphasis on aptitude tests and interview results. Thus, in addition to principal interview findings, this section should include any available test results, such as mental ability, verbal ability, numerical ability, mechanical comprehension, or clerical aptitude. Interviews should also combine test and interview findings in such a way that they summarize the quality of the candidate's thinking. Items concerned with quality of thinking would of course be expressed in such terms as "analytical ability," "ability to plan and organize," "criticalness of thinking," and "intellectual breadth and depth."

In writing the summary of assets and shortcomings, interviewers should select items of particular importance in terms of the job for which the candidate is being considered. In addition to listing appropriate items of ability, personality, motivation, and character, they should always note the relevance of the candidate's work history and educational preparation.

WRITING THE OVERALL SUMMARY

In completing the overall summary of the Interview Rating Form, the interviewer should write a brief description of the candidate's qualifications for the job in question. This takes the form of three paragraphs—the first paragraph devoted to a summation of the candidate's principal assets, a second paragraph that describes the most serious shortcomings, and a third paragraph in which interviewers seek to resolve the major assets and shortcomings in such a way that they show whether the assets outweigh the shortcomings or vice versa. And, in this third and final paragraph, interviewers show how they arrived at their overall rating.

The three paragraphs of the overall summary will draw upon the summary of assets and the summary of shortcomings that appear above. There will be some obvious redundancy, but every effort should be made to word the summary in such a way that the individual seems to "come to life" as a unique person. An example of an appropriately worded overall summary appears below.

> Harry Ritter deserves great credit for what he has been able to make of himself in view of what he has had to work with. Without much in the way of early financial, educational, or cultural advantages, he has managed to attain a very good record of achievement both in the army and at Elmer Electric. He has done this primarily as a result of his tremendous energy, his willingness to work hard and to put in long hours, and his ability to make maximum utilization of his abilities. In addition, Harry has some natural leadership ability as a result of his personal forcefulness, self-confidence, and tough-mindedness. Finally, his experience with Elmer Electric represents a strong plus in terms of his ability to fit in here.
>
> Negatively, Harry is not especially gifted intellectually, although his intelligence probably falls within the average range of the college population. Nor does he have a great amount of intellectual depth or breadth. He is more of a "doer" than a "thinker." The kind of person who tends to push people

a bit too hard, Harry needs to develop more tact and social sensitivity.

Harry Ritter's assets clearly outweigh his shortcomings—to the point that he represents a very good candidate for the first level of supervision in the manufacturing function. He has a rather ideal personality for production supervision in the sense that he is at his best when he can "put out the day-to-day fires" and "move the pieces out the door." Harry should be able to progress to the middle management level without much difficulty, but it is somewhat doubtful that his intellectual capacity will carry him much beyond that point.

MAKING THE OVERALL RATING

The interviewer will be guided by the extent to which the candidate's assets outweigh liabilities, or vice versa. No candidate is expected to possess all the qualifications listed in the worker specifications for a given job. The interviewer's task is to weigh the strength of the candidate's assets against the severity of his or her shortcomings, evaluate how much the candidate's shortcomings are likely to be a handicap in the job under consideration, and estimate the extent to which the individual's assets should lead to a successful job performance.

Assets of considerable strength may compensate for certain shortcomings. For example, in some cases strong motivation, relevant work experience, and good intellectual qualifications may compensate for below-average educational preparation. In such instances, an "above average" overall rating might be justified, despite the "below average" rating on education and training.

However, certain liabilities may be so damaging to the candidate's cause that they disqualify the individual regardless of the number of favorable ratings in other categories. A candidate lacking in honesty and sincerity or one exceedingly immature would undoubtedly merit a low overall rating despite the number of high ratings that may have been given in other important areas. Interviewers should be guided by one further consideration—the candidate's potential for further growth and development. Although the candidate's qualifications for a given job may be only "average" at the present time, he or she may be a person of such potential that the candidate could one day become a most productive employee.

FURTHER USES OF THE COMPLETED INTERVIEW RATING FORM

In the case of those individuals who are hired, the completed Interview Rating Form becomes an important part of the employee's permanent file. And since shortcomings have been carefully recorded, this information can become the basis for the employee's further development. Apprised of the new employee's developmental needs, supervisors can take immediate steps to help the employee, beginning the first day of the job.

The completed Interview Rating Form also can provide the basis for follow-up studies designed to improve the selection procedures. The overall interviewer rating can subsequently be compared with performance on the job. Such follow-up information helps interviewers identify their own interviewing weaknesses and makes it possible for them to work to eliminate these weaknesses in their future discussions with other candidates. Moreover, follow-up studies of this kind enable the employment manager to evaluate the interviewing staff, in terms of both additional training needs and possible reassignment to other employment functions.

Part Four

Additional Applications of Interview Techniques

Chapter Fourteen | The Campus Interview

The campus interview deserves special attention because it represents a company's greatest opportunity to recruit truly outstanding young people. However, because campus recruiters are usually forced to crowd some 12 to 15 interviews into a single day, the task is both difficult and enervating. Recruiters discover that they can devote no more than 30 minutes to each student—20 minutes to the interview itself, five minutes to the interview report, and five minutes to prepare for the next student. This means that recruiters have only a scant 20 minutes to decide whether a given student merits further consideration. That's why the more sophisticated companies send some of their best people to the colleges and train them thoroughly in intensive interviewing.

Continuation of the interview process involves travel expense to company headquarters and subsequent interviews by several important and highly paid people in the organization. This costs a company more money than most people realize. A great deal is riding on each decision a recruiter makes on campus before the candidate is brought in.

PREPARATION

Careful examination of each student's résumé prior to the interview can pay big dividends. Such study, for example, can reveal the extent to which the individual has any concentration of courses or internship and/or practical work experience that fits the recruiter's job description. A student's extracurricular activities might suggest qualities of leadership. Examination of the personal history résumé can help recruiters decide where they might spend the most time and where they should probe for more information.

As the Campus Interview Guide on pages 173-174 suggests, these interviews should begin with small talk, usually based on some special award or achievement. Recruiters should search for such a topic in the résumé and prepare a three-part question. If they discover, for example, that a student has won a prize for mathematics, they might formulate such a question as: "I am impressed that you won the Hogue Mathematics Prize. Tell me what the competition was like, what preparation you made, and what the award has meant to you."

Or, if no special awards appear on the résumé, it is often helpful to ask the student to compare life in his or her hometown with life in the college area: "I noticed that you grew up in Peoria. How would you contrast life there with living in Boston—with respect to attitudes of the people, cost of living, climate, educational opportunities?"

Beginning questions like these—introduced casually and with appropriate facial expressions—tend to put the interviewee at ease and encourage the person to talk at some length.

THE 20-MINUTE INTERVIEW

It is especially important in this short discussion to encourage the interviewee to do most of the talking. This is accomplished by rapport-inducing techniques discussed earlier: small talk, lead questions, facial and vocal expressions, the calculated pause, reinforcement, and playing down of negative information. The box on the next two pages provides a guide for the campus interview.

Since the educational experience is often the most important expe-

Campus Interview Guide

Begin the interview with small talk, which can begin with a three-part question: "I am impressed that you won the Hillard award. Tell me what you had to do to win that award, what the competition was like, and what it meant to you."

Then: "Let me tell you about our discussion today. In our company we believe that the more I can learn about you the better able I will be to place you in a job that makes the best use of your abilities. So, today, I would like to have you tell me everything you can about your education and a little about your work experience. Let's start with your education."

Education

Subject Preferences. "What subjects have you liked best in college? What is there about those subjects that appeals to you?" *(Probing for an indication about analytical thinking)*

Grades. "What about grades in college? Are they average, above average, or perhaps a little below average? If you know, what is your class rank?"

College Boards. "What were your SAT scores—verbal and math?"

Extracurricular Activities (sports, offices held, music, clubs). "Beyond your class work, what activities have you participated in?"

Effort. "How conscientious a student are you? Have you worked about as hard as the average student, a little harder, or perhaps not quite as hard?"

Colleges Applied to. "What colleges did you apply to? Which ones accepted you?"

Work History

Lead Question. "Did you have any jobs during high school or college that you think added materially to your growth and development?"

Likes and Dislikes. "Did you get a performance appraisal on that job? What traits or abilities did your supervisor like about you? What traits did your supervisor think needed further development?"

If No Performance Appraisal, Say: "If there had been an appraisal, what traits or abilities do you think your supervisor would have liked about you? What traits do you think your supervisor would have said needed further development?"

Terminate the Interview: "You have given me a fine picture of your background and it is clear that you have many important strengths that will help you in the future. Thank you very much for talking with me today."

Notes to Interviewer

At the Beginning of the Interview. By means of frequent reinforcement, facial expressions, and "playing down" of negative information, try to get the student to do most of the talking. Place a small clock on the table immediately in front of you and refer to it frequently in order to keep the interview to 20 minutes. Look at this Guide constantly and use all of the questions verbatim and in the indicated order.

At the End of the Interview. Take the time to sell your company only to those students you wish to recommend for a site visit. Drawing upon information from Figure 13-1 in Chapter 13 on Personality and Ability, write a few paragraphs on each student.

rience people in their early 20s have had, it is wise to spend the major portion of the 20 minutes on college background—perhaps as much as 15 minutes. This gives interviewers an ample opportunity to discuss the educational background in depth. When time is limited, it is better to discuss one important area of the interview in genuine depth than to spread oneself too thin by trying to cover all of the areas.

If one covers all of the questions found on the Campus Interview Guide verbatim and in the indicated order, abundant clues to mental ability, motivation, and maturity will normally come to light. Clues to mental ability, for example, should emerge from discussion of grades, effort required to get the grades, SAT scores, response to depth questions, and academic standards of schools attended.

Clues to motivation can often be found in such factors as the decision to embark on a difficult college major, effort expended on studies (late evening study and study on weekends), and participation in extracurricular activities such as a grueling sport. The latter activities provide valid clues to energy and stamina.

Clues to maturity can be found in the kind of judgment exercised in such major decisions as choice of college, choice of college major, and how the student expects to utilize the major after college graduation. The level of maturity can also be assessed by noting the extent to which the student was able to "put first things first" by concentrating on studies first rather than becoming too distracted by time-demanding extracurricular affairs.

PROBING FOR CLUES TO BEHAVIOR

Utilization of the Two-Step Probing Question should result in appreciable evidence of analytical and critical thinking. This technique, of course, is designed to probe for the "why" of the various decisions the student has made during his or her college career.

When probed for the reason behind the choice of college, one student might say, "Because it had such a beautiful campus and because I was so favorably impressed with the people I met on my first day there." Another student might reply, "It was because I had learned that this college has the best department in aeronautical engineering on the East Coast, and that the faculty here is top notch."

It is also a good idea ask how students went about choosing their college major. One student might say, "Oh, I guess I just drifted into it. I liked the teachers and found the subject easy." Another student might say, "I chose biology because it is a very orderly and systematic science, and I guess I am that way. In these days of burgeoning biogenetics, an undergraduate degree in biology represents a great springboard for interesting graduate work."

The second reply in each case represents a far more mature reaction.

Exploring Work Experience

Because there will be so little time left to talk about work experience—perhaps as little as five minutes—it is obviously impossible to touch upon all of a student's summer and after-school jobs. It is a better idea to encourage students to relate their single most important work experience: "Have you had any jobs in high school or college that you think added materially to your growth and development?" Most every student has had at least one such experience and is usually anxious to talk about it.

The interviewer then guides the student through a discussion of likes, dislikes, number of hours worked, and how that particular experience stimulated development. This discussion culminates in questions about the results of the performance appraisals. Here, it is important not to be satisfied with one or two strengths or development needs. Say, "What other traits did your supervisor like about you?" and "What other traits did your supervisor say you needed to improve?"

The All-Important Factor of Control

Interviewers will find that the only way to keep the campus interview within 20 minutes is to place a small clock immediately in front of them and to refer to it every two or three minutes. This requires stiff discipline, but it is the only way to process some 12 to 15 students in a single day. With practice, interviewers will be quick to pick up any tendency to over elaborate and move the student along to another topic. And they will do this by interrupting with appropriate timing.

Interviewers also need to control the discussion in such a way that they get more *evaluative* as opposed to *descriptive* information. And they need to concentrate on getting hard data. This means that they should ask for quantification wherever that is possible—number of hours worked on a given job, class standing (if known), how late the student studies normally at night and how many hours are put in on weekend study, and, when a student indicates long hours spent on a part-time job while attending school, how many credit hours were taken simultaneously.

SELLING THE COMPANY

Many campus interviewers make a big mistake by concentrating their major efforts on selling the company rather than on evaluating the individual student. This is not to say, however, that selling the company does not represent an important factor. Many companies will vie for what they consider "the best student" and they will offer every possible inducement. Obviously, then, the sales pitch represents an important aspect of the campus interview. But, as we shall subsequently see, this should be introduced at the very end of the interview—after the student has been evaluated.

Some companies try to get a leg up on their competition by scheduling an evening discussion prior to their subsequent interviews with individual students. This procedure is highly recommended since it removes some of the sales burden from the individual interviews. Evening discussions provide a great opportunity for explanation of company policies, training programs, wage structure, opportunities for advancement, and the like. And "Question and Answer" periods can result in a great deal more information than the interviewer could possibly have time to discuss in the interview itself.

THE INSUFFICIENTLY QUALIFIED STUDENT

Interviewers who see some 15 students in a given day will probably find only three or four they consider sufficiently qualified for further consideration. This means that in the vast majority of cases there is no real need for a big sales job. In the case of those students who are not to be recommended, interviewers can pass out any printed company material, thank students for their interest, and tell them that they will be hearing from the company within the next few weeks. They can also take the time to answer any immediate questions quickly. This brief windup gives the interviewers a few minutes of much needed rest prior to seeing the next student and helps them husband their energies and maintain their sanity in an otherwise impossible day.

THE QUALIFIED STUDENT

When interviewers determine that a student is qualified for further consideration, they can "pull out all the stops" in their effort to kindle interest in their companies. And, because we have placed the sales function at the end of the interview, they are in a position to sell specifically rather than generally. For example, when they have determined that a given candidate has a compelling interest in developing computer software, they can describe in detail the company's computer software development program and spell out potential for upward mobility in that area. Or, in the case of students with demonstrated leadership ability, they can emphasize the extent to which their companies provide early opportunity for people with genuine leadership ability. By positioning the sales function at the end of the interview, interviewers give themselves more breathing space.

THE INTERVIEW REPORT

In general, campus recruiters do a very poor job of recording interview results. Sometimes, they only make a few check marks on a form that has very little meaning in the first place. And some recruiters even wait until they have seen several students before they try to record results on the ones they decide to recommend.

The sample campus interview report, which is shown in the box on pages 179-180, embodies the kind of information that is possible to obtain by an experienced interviewer within a 20-minute period. Of course, reports such as this cannot be written without some prior training.

Before beginning their reports, interviewers will find it helpful to refer again to the Personality and Ability lists from Figure 13-1 in Chapter 13. We suggest that this page be copied and placed under a sheet of clear plastic for ready reference. In addition to recording the extent to which a given candidate measures up to certain aspects of the job description, interviewers can also record qualifications in terms of such important factors as maturity, motivation, intelligence, leadership, and people skills.

Daniel

It will be clear from this short interview that Dan's accomplishments to date have come as a result of incredible motivation. And these accomplishments are impressive: Tau Beta Pi, outstanding physics award, and high grades in high school and college. To do this he studied 40 to 50 hours a week in college—including many all-nighters—and regularly studied on weekends. Unquestionably, Dan possesses great energy, stamina, and willingness to work.

It also seems apparent that Dan is strong technically. He has a high math aptitude (650 SAT math score), has been keenly interested in mechanical engineering since he was a small boy, and seems to have a high mechanical aptitude (proud of his ability to tear down the engine of his car and put it back together). Over the past four summers he has acquired relevant engineering experience from his intern experiences at Northrop. During these summers, he has developed a reputation for reliability, hard work, and hands-on expertise.

Dan's principal shortcomings stem from his low verbal aptitude. His SAT verbal score of 415 is quite low; he has always had trouble with English, and his current advisors are critical of his writing skills. From the interview, it also became apparent that Dan's vocabulary is limited and that he is not very articulate.

There is also reason to believe that Dan tends to be a one-dimensional person. He has put so much effort into study and summer work that there has been little time for anything else (no extracurricular activities in college). And he has not developed socially to the extent that many others of his age have. Nor is he very sophisticated intellectually.

In summary, Dan is the classic case of the overachiever, one who attains results primarily on the basis of hard work. He does not have a first-class intellect, nor is there much evidence of leadership. There are further clues to lack of self-confidence (the need to stay close to home). Dan deserves great credit for what he has managed to accomplish and gives the appearance of being a wonderful human being. He can be recommended for further consideration as a direct hire but does not seem to represent a top candidate for the Carter Training Program (a program that costs the company some $100,000 per person and seeks to recruit only the "cream of the crop").

One might ask: "What are the reservations about hiring an over-achiever—someone who will work very hard to accomplish what is expected of him?" The answer is that there are no reservations about hiring such a person for a *specialized* assignment where high potential for advancement is not an important requisite. But many overachievers do have a strong drive for upward mobility, and the time will surely come when such individuals discover that hard work alone will not be enough to solve the complex problems that confront upper-level management. Nor will they be able to draw upon the generalized thinking that represents such an important requirement for success at the top.

Chapter Fifteen	# Conducting Performance Appraisals and Giving Feedback

Because the feedback of appraisal information involves an interview, every single technique of the evaluation interview is applicable in this procedure—the rapport-inducing techniques, the probing techniques, and even the techniques for control of the interview. Managers who have trained in interviewing have an enormous advantage in terms of using feedback to enhance performance, confront lack of performance, and shape behavior.

THE CONCEPT

Feedback is the process of communication whereby managers share with employees their view of strengths and shortcomings. This sharing should be done in a way that lays the groundwork for behavioral change. Employees must be able to "hear" and understand the feedback. The well-trained manager must realize that feedback has two distinct parts—first, to reinforce existing positive behavior and, second, to discuss negative behavior as a prelude to future growth and development.

Traditionally, feedback has been a difficult experience for both managers and employees. In a recent study, 4,000 employees in 190

181

firms were surveyed concerning reactions to the feedback process in their companies. A full 70 percent reported that their managers did not give them a clear picture of what was expected of them, and only 20 percent said their performance was reviewed at all. This provides clear evidence that feedback is not used as an effective management tool on a consistent basis. And when it is not used with sufficient frequency, neither party feels comfortable in the sharing situation.

Some people who do not receive appraisals or feedback may develop negative feelings toward their managers, believing they are not fulfilling their management responsibilities. In some cases, lack of performance feedback can cause anxiety and frustration. It may even lower efficiency and productivity.

When feedback appraisals are awkwardly given—as is so often the case—the discussion can become emotionally charged. For example, individuals may take a defensive stance in reaction to the discussion of shortcomings, and this can be uncomfortable for both parties. But, where feedback appraisals are competently handled from the top down, this often produces a "trickle down" effect. Getting effective performance feedback from one's superior makes it easier to conduct this same kind of quality performance with one's subordinates. And this type of communication can help avoid duplication of work, overlapping authority, unclear performance standards, unclear job assignments, and ambiguous goals.

FEEDBACK—A SHARED RESPONSIBILITY

Feedback is usually seen as the responsibility of the manager or appraiser. But, in the most effective feedback, the recipient plays a more active role than simply being the passive receiver; in addition to being open to receiving feedback, employees should seek out this kind of information—expressly ask for it.

There is also a need for people to share information about themselves so the appraiser can place the feedback in proper context, by putting it in a form that has the most meaning for the recipient. Hence, the information concerning short-term and long-term goals, factors of job satisfaction, how much and what kind of supervision they prefer, what talents they feel they have that they are not utilizing, and how they feel about their present job—all these pieces of information can be most helpful to the manager. This is why an evaluation interview prior to the formal feedback session has so much meaning.

FEEDBACK–AN ONGOING PROCESS

The feedback review is not an event; it should be viewed as an ongoing process that embodies the concept of continuous development. Only in that way can it influence performance, benefiting both managers and subordinates. From a manager's perspective, it helps to maintain and improve current employee job performance. For employees, it answers the often unspoken question, "How am I doing?" and provides reassurance and helps boost morale.

Despite the fact that feedback should be an ongoing process, employees often receive very little of this. Many do not even get an annual review and, when they do, they frequently find the experience unsatisfactory. Managers shy away from feedback because they have been given little help in terms of how to provide it. We will therefore devote the rest of this chapter to the annual review, with the thought that, once managers learn how to do this comfortably, they will subsequently give more attention to the ongoing process.

PREPARATION–THE EMPLOYEE'S ROLE

There has been much more information published on the process of giving feedback than there has been on how to *receive* it. Yet, the latter is of equal importance. Both are necessary conditions for effective utilization of the process. Just as the manager plans for the feedback meeting, so should the employee. By assuming a positive attitude, the employee can expect to get a great deal more out of the experience. The following principles should prove helpful for employees at all levels:

- Try to view feedback as a process of continuous development—ongoing and dynamic. It should not be viewed as an isolated experience. Solicit feedback from managers on a regular and frequent basis. Taking the initiative to seek feedback creates some measure of control as opposed to the more passive approach of waiting until someone decides to give it. The act of seeking out this information conveys the message that this is important to you.

- Be prepared to share information about yourself—your short-term and long-term goals, the kind of work that provides the most satisfaction, and how you feel about your job.

- Try to be open and non-defensive. Try not to "explain away" negative feedback by merely saying to yourself, "Managers don't understand me." Blaming others is easy. Doing something about one's shortcomings is more difficult. It is important to listen and understand what is being said and to determine how you can benefit from the criticism.

- Maintain an open attitude toward the content of the feedback. This will maximize the chances that it will be constructive. Go into the interview with the idea of giving serious consideration to all suggestions and taking whatever action may be necessary to make this a positive experience. Develop a "can do" attitude.

- Take an active role in the interview. Discuss the feedback, ask questions, and seek clarification. When a point is made that does not ring true, do not be afraid to ask for additional evidence or documentation. In short, try to get as much information as possible before evaluating the meaning of the comments. Then, if you agree with the comments, acknowledge their value and let the manager know how you feel about what you are hearing. It might be well to say, "That has a lot of meaning for me and I can understand how I might profit from it." This reflects a far more positive attitude than simply sitting there with a blank stare.

- Be aware of possible nonverbal messages you may be transmitting with such factors as eye contact, facial expressions, gestures, and posture. Leaning back in the chair with your arms crossed, for example, may convey the message that feedback will be resisted despite any of your claims of openness. On the other hand, sitting forward conveys the message of interest, and nodding your head shows involvement and participation.

The Feedback Reaction Form shown in the box below provides employees with a helpful tool to use after the feedback session. Use of this form can help employees synthesize the feedback information, react to it in an intelligent way, and gain "ownership" of it. This form also forces the individual to reflect upon what has been shared. By writing reactions, individuals can begin to see those areas that need attention. They may even attempt to validate the manager's perception of strengths and development needs with some of the people who are closest to them and know them best. In this way, employees become both accountable and responsible for the feedback information.

Feedback Reaction Form

Areas of major strengths: _____

Areas I want to work on: _____

Observations I accept: _____

Observations I do not accept: _____

Things I want to think about: _____

Observations I do not understand: _____

How I feel right now: _____

PREPARATION—THE MANAGER'S ROLE

Feedback sessions present an opportunity to communicate to employees precisely where the organization is going, its longer-range future, and the potential fit with respect to the employee's skills and the organization's needs. The session tries to create an interdependency— an integration of the company's needs, the employee's needs, and a fit of the two.

In approaching the feedback meeting, managers should plan to tell employees to expect three types of information. They can expect to receive information that is familiar in the sense that they have heard it before and understand where it comes from. They can expect to receive information that is new and not readily understandable in terms of where it may fit in. And, finally, they may regard some of the information as irrelevant and without merit. By introducing feedback in this way, managers can reduce the employees' level of anxiety and help them remain open to the process.

The following principles should prove helpful:

- Be prepared to document from the employee's job performance every single item you plan to convey. If you are not in a position to provide this kind of documentation for a given item—whether it represents a strength or shortcoming—it has no place on your list. If you plan to discuss a need for better organization, for example, you should be able to provide documentation such as the following: "Do you remember when you began work on the Z project two months ago? We had to interrupt after three days and ask you to start over, utilizing a different action plan. I suggested then that that was a matter of prioritizing and organization. Yesterday I had to ask you to rewrite one of your reports, using a different plan and procedure. Wasn't that also a matter of organization?"

- Keep a record of each employee's performance so that specific examples of both positive and negative performance can be cited. If you plan to tell a person that she tends to be "overly dominant," you should be able to cite several incidents such as "In yesterday's meeting you had a tendency to do most of the talking and relatively little listening. As a result, other people did not feel involved or did not feel they had an opportunity to express their own opinions."

- Plan to be specific rather than general. Too often employees leave feedback meetings without a sense of what occurred, because the discussion was too general and nonspecific. As a result, they either dismiss what they have heard or do not take ownership for the situation.

- A manager may say, for example, "Your speech was OK, but you left out bits of information that might have strengthened your presentation." An employee may wonder what was effective in the presentation and what specifically he could have done to make it better. A more effective feedback statement might have been "The aspects of your presentation that were effective included your visual presentation, handouts, and discussion points. On the other hand, you needed to bring in factual data to support your position." When you are candid and frank, you leave nothing to the imagination.

- Remember that feedback must be limited to those factors within the individual's control. Most people are understandably resistant when criticized for something they are powerless to change or improve, such as mental ability, nervousness, or some aspects of personal appearance. To be told that one is not all that sharp or intelligent, for example, can be a devastating experience.

- You should plan to state the objectives of the performance review—the extent to which the information will be used for salary increases, training needs, morale building, or simply to enhance performance. There should also be an agreement between employee and manager on goals, the standards by which performance will be measured, and what constitutes "superior performance."

- Remember that the intent of feedback is to help people, not to hurt them. Some managers, unfortunately, like to use feedback as a leverage or power tool—to build themselves up at the expense of others.

- The review should be regarded as an opportunity for you to offer guidance, encouragement, and suggestions for improvement. You should plan to use it as a means for developing a set of constructive plans to strengthen identified weak areas and help people grow and develop their full potential.

- Plan to focus the discussion on behavior rather than on the person. Instead of telling an employee that he is rigid or inflexible, it is better to point out situations in which such behavior has occurred: "In our team discussion, you tended to reiterate your point of view over and over again as opposed to adopting a more open attitude."

- The process should be as much counseling and coaching as it is evaluation—as much a listening as a talking activity. Ask questions to clarify what has been said. Keep the focus on the employee. Active listening requires full attention. Make it clear that you consider this meeting important. One important objective is to increase motivation and self-esteem. Make it a "we," not a "you" discussion.

- You should plan to make your feedback candid and frank. If work has been less than satisfactory, you must acknowledge this. You must be prepared to give honest criticism so employees know where they stand. If employees have some concern about your level of honesty, they begin to wonder about possible hidden agendas.

- Probe more deeply for needs and motivations in order to gain additional insight concerning those reporting to you. Ask such questions as "Where does your drive for achievement come from? Do you feel a need to be competitive or is it a drive for accomplishment? What satisfies you about your job? Some people look for security, financial rewards, or personal recognition. What is important to you?"

Although this discussion is primarily about the formal evaluation interview, it is important for managers to remember that feedback should ideally occur informally whenever it is appropriate. The following points address this process.

- Remember that feedback should be appropriately timed. Immediate feedback is best. Actually, it should be delayed only to avoid embarrassing an employee in front of others or to get more information about a particular situation. Comments should not be saved for a later formal setting. Employees cannot be expected to improve if they do not know that a problem exists. Informal feedback is a powerful tool since it provides a constant reminder that performance matters. An appropriate reminder: "I am pleased that you brought this project to a close under budget. That is quite an accomplishment! Is there something we can learn from your experience?"

- You should conduct reviews both formally and informally, and there should be continuous feedback about results. However, too much feedback may be viewed as overly close supervision or control. Even so, ongoing feedback is most effective when people have clearly defined job objectives and a means of measuring their own job performance.

The more formal annual review should become a summary of all the pieces of recognition the employee has accumulated throughout the year. In this way, the annual review will hold few surprises and will be less traumatic and more meaningful.

Finally, the proper person from management should be selected to conduct the formal review session, and this person must possess sufficient credibility and power to make the session productive. Credibility comes from the extent to which employees believe the manager has enough first-hand information to evaluate their performance. Actually, credibility is a function of two factors—expertise and trust. In addition to being considered trustworthy, the manager must be perceived as possessing the expertise to judge behavior accurately, and this, of course, means a familiarity with the task itself and the employee's own performance of that task. Power represents the means of controlling valued results. In general, the higher the power of the source of feedback, the more likely the recipient will try to respond positively. This influences the extent to which employees accurately perceive the feedback and resolve to try to do something about it.

TYPES OF FEEDBACK

There are several different types of feedback. Each serves a different purpose and is suited for particular situations.

Tell and listen. In this type of feedback, the manager assumes a more passive role while the employee clarifies, explains, and acknowledges the feedback. Example: "You have told me that my handling of the meeting yesterday was too directive and that I didn't allow other people sufficient opportunity for input. Let me give you some background on why I used more authority than is usual for me." While this approach has merit in some situations, it places full responsibility on the employee and limits the manager's effectiveness as a coach and mentor.

Tell and sell. After feedback is given, the manager discusses its value and usefulness, maintaining an active role by talking about how an employee might improve performance. Example: "The reports you write are not condensed enough. It is difficult to find the important facts and figures. You need to become aware of the importance we place on concise, well-organized reports. Look at this report and see where you might cut and improve it."

In this type of session, the manager is more active and the employee is more passive. The "selling" by the manager may be a turnoff to the employee, and the only reason for change may be to please the manager. This may bring short-term change, but not necessarily long-term improvement. In a sense, the manager is mandating or dictating the necessary improvement. Commitment on the part of the employee is therefore minimized.

Problem-solving approach. This involves a joint relationship, with the manager and the employee working together in order to understand the problem and how to solve it. Example: "Our department has had trouble the past two months reaching production figures. Let's go over what we have been doing and try to see where the problem is. In particular, the people in your area seem to be absent more than is usual. What do you believe is going on?" Generally, the most effective feedback session is one where both manager and employee participate fully. This approach sets the stage for longer-lasting change to occur and for the employee to feel the manager is vested in the improvement goals and, at the same time, is concerned for his well-being.

FORMAL ANNUAL REVIEW

We have pointed out the value of interview training as a prelude to feedback. At the same time, we realize that many managers will not have received this training. Even so, they can profit from techniques of the evaluation interview discussed in Parts Two and Three of this book. In this section, therefore, we will call attention to some of these techniques and show how they can not only make the manager and employee more comfortable in the feedback session, but also help to make the review a more positive and constructive experience.

The Importance of Building Rapport

Since the initial purpose of the annual review is to get the employee to feel at ease, open up, and participate extensively in the discussion, the manager should draw upon all the rapport-inducing techniques described earlier—small talk, the calculated pause, facial expressions, positive reinforcement (verbal and nonverbal), and partial playing down of negative information. Only when rapport has been established can the employee be expected to "hear" what is being said, as a result of minimizing filters of defensiveness and other "emotional noise."

This interview should begin in much the same way any other interview should begin—with small talk. In the course of seating herself and throwing out the question informally and with an appropriate smile, the manager might say, "I know that you participate in our fitness center. I think that's great! Tell me about your routine and what you think the experience is doing for you." By encouraging the subordinate to talk for two or three minutes about this extraneous topic, the manager not only begins the interview in a pleasant, nonthreatening manner, but also subtly conveys the impression that she expects the employee to do a good bit of the talking.

With the small talk concluded, the manager discusses the purpose of the review and encourages the employee to discuss factors of job satisfaction and both short-term and long-term goals: "Let me tell you a little about our discussion today. As you know, we get together once a year to summarize what has happened to you over the past 12 months in terms of your achievements and opportunities for further development. But, I believe I can be more helpful to you if you tell me a little about your short-term and long-term goals and the aspects of any job that give you the most satisfaction. Let's start with the latter. What does a job have to have to give you satisfaction? Some people look for money, some for security; some want to manage, some want to create. What's important to you?"

Once the manager has discussed factors of job satisfaction, the kind of job the employee would like next, and where he sees himself five years hence, the manager is ready for the core of the interview—strengths and development needs.

Strengths

We always begin this section of the review with a discussion of strengths. This permits us to accent the positive at the very start and helps the recipient to understand his importance to the organization and how much he is valued. Few people have done a very good job of evaluating their strengths and some may even feel somewhat self-conscious about reviewing them. This often stems from early upbringing, which may have instilled the dictum, "Don't blow your own horn." At any rate, the manager may ease this situation by borrowing the question on strengths from the Interview Guide: "Let's begin by highlighting some of your major accomplishments over the past year. Do you think you have worked harder than the average person, organized things better, gotten along with other people better, given more attention to detail—just what?"

As each asset surfaces, the manager should "build up" or emphasize the importance to the organization of that strength, provided she agrees with it: "Attention to detail is an all-important asset to this company; we are all striving for zero errors!" By developing a sizable list of strengths and accenting the importance of each one, the manager begins to build a psychological advantage, in the sense that the employee will subsequently be more willing to disclose shortcomings now that he knows his supervisor is aware of all his good points and values his accomplishments.

The manager should "stay with" the discussion of strengths for a considerable period, "priming the pump" from the list of strengths she has prepared on that particular individual prior to the review session. Some managers tend to rush through this discussion in order to get to areas that need improvement. This is a big mistake, since it not only fails to build self-esteem and boost morale, but also makes it subsequently more difficult to stage a constructive discussion of shortcomings.

Be sure to tie in strengths to job performance. It is not enough to tell a person that you know he is a hard worker. It is much more meaningful to say, "I appreciate all the hard work and overtime hours you spent in order to complete the Zan project on schedule. I know that involved a lot of self-sacrifice and support from your family as well."

Development Needs

After the discussion of strengths has been completed, the session should focus on areas where performance was below expectations. As indicated earlier, it is crucial for the manager to have prepared thoroughly for this part of the interview prior to the session. She must be able to document each shortcoming with examples and hard data gleaned from job performance during the period of the review. This is important because it is human nature to try to improve only in those areas where one is convinced of the need to improve.

Here again, we can borrow the question on development needs from the Interview Guide: "You certainly have an impressive array of strengths. Now let's talk a bit about some of the things you could improve. You know none of us is perfect; we all have traits or abilities that can stand improvement. And the person who becomes aware of such traits is in a position to do something about them and, hence, to grow and develop a lot faster than might otherwise have been the case. What are some of the areas you think you could improve?"

In response to this question, the employee may volunteer several of the items on the manager's list. Each item should be completely discussed and the conversation on each point should conclude with an agreed-upon action plan, with milestones for improvement and evaluation. This shows that the manager really wants to help, and it also establishes the fact that she expects the employee to improve. Make certain that you let the person know you have confidence in him even when he may have failed upon occasion to achieve what he has set out to do in the past: "I know that you will find a way to make the necessary changes so that this project will be completed and be as successful as your strong track record in project management indicates."

When the employee can think of no additional areas for improvement, the manager should introduce other items on her list one by one, using the evaluation interview's double-edged question: "What about firmness with people? Do you have as much of this as you would like to have, or is this something you could improve a little bit?"

When the employee says he sees no real need to improve this, the manager must supply documentation from her prepared material:

"Well, you have admitted to me from time to time that you have two people under your supervision who perform far less well than the rest of the group. Is it possible that you are giving these people too much benefit of the doubt when you really should have separated them? You know you mentioned earlier that you have aspirations for upper-level management, and all of us around here feel that mental toughness or the ability to make hard decisions about people represents one of the truly critical factors in functioning effectively on that level."

If the employee agrees at last that mental toughness does represent an area in which he could improve, the manager and subordinate must work out an action plan to influence this development. The manager might say, as one of her suggestions, "How would you feel about taking the company course in assertiveness training?" or, "Let's keep tabs on the absenteeism in your group and see if that can be improved over a period of time."

As implied above, there is little point to giving negative feedback unless this is accompanied by specific suggestions as to how the individual might go about making the necessary behavioral change. The manager and employee should work together to create a developmental action plan. Such a plan is crucial, since it represents the link between feedback and how the individual can expect to make the appropriate changes. A constructive feedback review might come up with four or five areas for self-growth and improvement, together with steps necessary to facilitate the change. To cite another example, let us assume that better presentation skills have been identified as an area for improvement. In this case, the developmental action plan might include such specific steps as taking a course in effective presentation skills, videotaping one of the individual's presentations, or observing a presentation of some other person who is considered expert in this area.

End the Feedback on a Positive Note

The manager should always conclude the review on a positive note. A brief summary at the end should list the most important strengths and the fact that these are highly valued. "You certainly have an impressive array of strengths. I depend on you to provide the creative input we need in this department, and I depend on your unique ability to see that things get done."

The manager should also ask the employee to provide his own summary of what he has heard. If the person is missing something important, ask questions to get at the facts. Listen carefully for evidence that the individual really understands the problem areas and intends to do something constructive about them.

Focus on the future. Feedback should present an opportunity for future successes. The crucial question is "How can we set things up so that you can do an even better job next time?" Forward-looking questions are positive and reflect promise for continued improvement.

Nonverbal Feedback

Since most psychologists now agree that nonverbal signals represent an important aspect of communication, no discussion of feedback would be complete without some attention to this factor. It has been our experience, in fact, that the nonverbal factor plays a significant, though often unrecognized, role. Nonverbal feedback involves body language and other cues that are used—often unconsciously—to express interest or to convey lack of attention. Some of the more common types of nonverbal communication include the following:

- **Appearance.** What "message" does your clothing convey? Authority? Informality? Does your appearance fit the occasion?
- **Gestures.** What are your hands saying? Clenched hands often symbolize tension and nervousness. Curled fists may indicate anger. Hands in pockets may portray resignation.
- **Posture.** Does your posture fit your verbal message? Are you leaning forward in interest toward the person or pushing back in your chair to keep at a distance? Frequent shifting of positions may be interpreted as impatience or lack of interest.
- **Eye Contact and Facial Expression.** Is the eye contact you maintain one of interest or a glare of intimidation? Does your facial expression betray a negative feeling despite the words you are using?
- **Voice.** Does the intonation, volume, and rate of speech reflect

the mood you wish to induce? Speaking too loudly, for example, may tend to intimidate the other person, causing that person to "clam up" rather than "speak up."

Awareness of all the factors involved in effective feedback enhances the probability that this important function will be given and received constructively. Creation of a base of open communication and trust stimulates managers and employees to engage in feedback regularly, thereby making continuous improvement a reality. The more formal feedback review, then, becomes a summary discussion of shared perceptions of past performance and results, a vehicle for developmental goals, and a chance to share the vision of the future.

Chapter Sixteen | Team Building

I n order to compete more effectively in the global market-place, we must begin to work toward a team-based style of management, where the whole is greater than all of the individual efforts combined. Hence, those companies that compete by integrating the talent and creativity of all of their employees will gain the competitive edge.

Individuals working together can create something very special. In sports, for example, we can look back at the United States hockey team in the 1980 Olympics. A group of amateur players came together as a team and won the gold medal by defeating the professionals on the Soviet hockey team, evermore known as the "Miracle on Ice." Individually, there were no superstars, but they came together with a common goal and with individual roles to support each other.

TRUST, OPENNESS, AND HONESTY–THE INDISPENSABLE ELEMENTS OF TEAM BUILDING

Little time has traditionally been spent on relations and trust building in the initial stages of team development. Groups were so task-oriented that there was a single-minded focus on specific outcomes. As a result, decision-making often got caught up in "hidden agendas" and the need for control and power.

It is widely recognized today, however, that early emphasis on rapport building pays big dividends. And this is where the techniques of the evaluation interview can play a big part—techniques such as reinforcement, playing down negative information, the calculated pause, and facial expressions. These techniques help team members listen to each other more closely. Gradually, relationships are built based on trust, openness, and honesty.

RISK-TAKING AND OPENNESS TO NEW IDEAS

It is easy to fall back on tried and true approaches and to evaluate alternatives on the basis of what we know, instead of trying something new. But if teams are to move forward as a whole, there has to be an element of risk-taking and openness to new ideas. There must be a climate where people can fail and not be judged poorly for taking a chance. If a team is to be creative, people must be willing to generate seemingly crazy ideas, even if they do not seem appropriate at the time. New strategies emerge only in climates where there is a willingness to change and adapt to new situations.

Team members must share their perceptions of themselves and invite perceptions of others to see how closely they match. People learn to expose themselves to other members of the team by sharing information about them and responding to probing questions. This can be a rather delicate process and may require the services of a knowledgeable consultant, skilled in the techniques of the evaluation interview.

The consultant may decide to administer the Myers-Briggs Type Indicator, an instrument that indicates basic preferences. The results produce neither right nor wrong preferences, but simply reflect different kinds of people who are interested in different things, may be drawn to different fields of work, and may even find it hard to understand each other. According to Isabel Briggs Myers (*Introduction to Type*), the Myers-Briggs Type Indicator "is primarily concerned with the valuable differences in people that result from where they like to focus their attention, the way they like to take in information, the way they like to decide, and the kind of lifestyle they adopt." Each type has its own inherent strengths and weaknesses.

The information resulting from the Myers-Briggs Type Indicator is shared with each team member individually, then the group is divided into subgroups. Members of each subgroup take turns leaving the room while those remaining jointly decide what they perceive as that person's style and basic personality traits. The individual then reenters and the subgroup compares the results of the Myers-Briggs Type Indicator with their joint assessment of that person. This exercise continues until each member has been through this experience. Individual reaction is understandably uneasy in the beginning, but people gradually warm to the experience and subsequently report that this is the first time they have ever had candid feedback from their peers and that they find it very constructive.

The second step of the feedback process focuses on having individuals tell some personal experiences about themselves. Experience has shown that this exercise helps people grow closer together. A questionnaire such as the one shown in the box on page 200 can be used to stimulate this discussion. Here again, the two-step probing question—an important element of the evaluation interview—can be used to advantage in developing additional information from each of these questions.

As team members get to know each other through feedback, they develop confidence in each other as well as mutual trust. Such confidence and trust enhances open and free-flowing communications, participative decision-making, and increased productivity through collective group effort. Only then can the team focus on creating a common goal to achieve desired outcomes. Results of high-performing teams can include:

- **Output**—where the team sets high output or high quality standards and regularly achieves them.
- **Objectives**—where the team shares in the understanding of the purpose and the mission; members learn to cooperate with one another and have a team spirit.

- **Energy**—where there is a strength that members share with one another.
- **Structure**—where the team develops its own operating style about making decisions, develops an understanding of individual roles and role responsibilities, and establishes the mechanics of setting the agenda items and evaluating their performance.
- **Atmosphere**—where there is a spirit that manifests itself in confidence and risk-taking, information-sharing, and open communication.
- **Autonomy**—where the results of team building are reflected in a high degree of control in the team's ability to make decisions.

Team Development Questionnaire

Directions: The list of questions below is designed to stimulate group discussion around work-related topics. The following ground rules should govern this discussion.

1. Take turns asking questions, either of specific individuals or of the group as a whole.
2. You must be willing to answer any question that is asked.
3. Work with the person who is answering to make certain that effective two-way understanding takes place.
4. All answers remain confidential within the group.

These questions may be asked in any order.

1. How do you feel about yourself in your present job?
2. What are you trying to accomplish in your work?
3. Where do you see yourself 10 years from now?
4. How are you perceiving me?
5. What would you predict to be my assessment of you?
6. What kind of working relationship do you want with me?
7. What factors in your job situation impede your goal accomplishment?
8. Where would you locate yourself on a 10-point scale of commitment to the goals of this group (1 is low, 10 is high)?
9. What personal growth efforts are you making?

Chapter Seventeen | Visioning

Would you tell me, please, which way I ought to go from here?"
"That depends a good deal on where you want to get to."
"Well, I don't really much care."
"Then, it doesn't matter which way you go."

These lines from Lewis Carroll's *Alice in Wonderland* could be applied to many business situations. The ability to create and implement a vision rests with our ability to probe and question where we are today and where we want to be in the future. The same kind of probing, open-ended questions we use in the interview can be put into practice here. Many companies, therefore, prefer to obtain the services of a consultant skilled in the techniques of the evaluation interview to help place the visioning process into operation.

QUESTIONS

The consultant meets with the head of the business unit involved and that person's immediate staff—usually eight to 10 people. Together they address questions such as the following:

- What are the critical dynamics of our organization's environment?
- How do things really work?
- To what degree are trends changing the nature of our industry, and does this pose opportunities or threats?
- How is our organization distinctive and unique?
- What is our potential as an organization, and where can we be five years from now?
- How would we feel about the vision we want to create? Would we want it if we could have it?

Of course these questions are only part of the analysis an organization needs to complete. But, if the analysis is thorough with respect to strengths and weaknesses as we see ourselves today, we stand a greater likelihood of developing opportunities with which to create tomorrow's reality. The effectiveness of any organization is based on the following principles:

- A stated purpose as to why the organization exists.
- A vision that inspires people to reach for what they could be and to rise above their fears and their preoccupations with current reality. This enables people to clarify and realize what they really want.
- Alignment of people to the vision, which in turn allows them to operate freely and fully as part of the larger whole. Alignment is not agreement; it deals with the more inspirational aspects of purpose and vision. Alignment indicates a common purpose and helps people transcend their differences.
- Empowerment that allows people and groups to take responsibility for and control of their lives. In such situations, people value personal power because they are committed to the same goal and direction. The increase in individual power increases total power of the organization.
- Results are achieved in truly meaningful ways because employees' goals are consistent with organizational goals.

DEVELOPING A VISION

Developing a vision for an organization is fundamental to its business results and people effectiveness. People need some framework to guide their day-to-day decisions and priorities. Visioning can provide an emotional appeal with which people can identify. It can focus on excellence, continuous improvement, and being better than the best. Visionary planning requires us to be insightful in answering the following six basic questions. Here the consultant draws upon two-step probing questions as in the evaluation interview to develop more complete and in-depth responses.

Where Are We Today? The importance of answering this question lies in the fact that only from our current knowledge can we build a foundation for the future. Answering this question shows us what we now have and leads to the next question: "What do we want to keep?" The reason to answer this question is to be sure that we carry forward what has worked in the past, i.e., "not throw the baby out with the bathwater."

Where Do We Want to Go? This is a fundamental question if we are to be all that we can be. We can envision what we want to create, but we must question and probe our assumptions more deeply if we are to achieve a vision of the future.

How Are We Going to Get There? Identifying a vision is only one phase of the visioning process. In order for the vision to be actualized, it must be implemented. Too often, lofty goals such as "excellence," "total quality," or "commitment to greatness" are set without the first steps toward those goals being identified.

When Will It Be Done? By placing a time frame on the planning and implementation of the process, we make a commitment to realizing the vision. Unfortunately, many times visioning gets stuck at the planning stages and is never implemented due to other priorities. Identification of benchmarks can help secure commitment and involvement.

Who Is Responsible for What? Commitment flows through involvement. And giving people a chance to participate in the process gives them a feeling of ownership. Making people responsible and accountable increases the likelihood of success.

How Much Will It Cost and What Are the Benefits? It is axiomatic that the benefits of any change must outweigh the costs in order for a desired change to take place. This is crucial if the visioning process is to have meaning.

When an organization has a clear sense of its purpose, direction, and desired future state, employees can better understand what the organization is trying to accomplish. When this vision is widely shared, people are better able to find their own roles. Everyone then gains a sense of importance.

SCENARIO EFFECTIVENESS TEST

The newly established vision should then be subjected to the Scenario Effectiveness Test. The answers to the test form the core understanding of the company's vision and how it will affect day-to-day operations.

- Does the definition of your vision make sense to a person unfamiliar with your company or division?
- Have you identified all the potential benefits and liabilities associated with your vision? Be sure you indicate both tangible and intangible opportunities and dangers.
- Have you quantified each opportunity and danger? Attach a dollar value to even the most intangible danger, such as a bad reputation.
- Does your scenario identify every key factor that will determine success or failure? Include less obvious environmental factors.
- Have you arranged the key success factors in order of decreasing priority? Be sure you can explain how each relates to the others.
- Have you properly sequenced all major events? Sometimes less critical events occur early, and in some cases events can take place concurrently.
- Do you understand the impact each major event will have on every other event? You should be able to describe how changes in one event will affect each of the other events.

- Have you weighed all the risks and costs of carrying out your vision, allowing for the unthinkable worst case?
- Does your scenario accommodate change?
- Can you commit your scenario to paper for further review and development?

ORGANIZATIONAL ANALYSIS

Any discussion of visioning must also, by its very nature, include discussion of organizational analysis. To expedite this process, the following criteria should be taken into consideration:

- What are the critical dynamics of our organization's environment? How do things really work? How do we make money?
- What trends are changing the nature of our industry? What represents the state of the art in the industry? Does it pose opportunities or threats?
- What do our customers really want? How do they value what we offer? Can we add greater value?
- Who are we as an organization? How do our people feel about who we are? How do they view our purpose?
- How is our organization distinctive and unique? What opportunities does our distinctiveness afford us?
- What are our most important and dominant capabilities, skills, and relationships? Can we further exploit them? Do we sufficiently understand them?
- What is our potential as an organization? Where can we be five years from now? If we did nothing different from what we are doing today, where would we be in five years?
- If I could rewrite the history of my own achievements or those of our industry, our organization, or our people, what would I change?
- Why have we succeeded in the past? Do I really understand the nature of and reasons for those successes?
- Why have we failed in the past? Do I really understand the reasons for those setbacks?

THE FINAL STEP

The final step in the visioning process is taking a second look at the organization as the visioning process takes root. The following key actions and questions provide a guide to this process:

- Reinvent what we do
  - What is our work?
  - Should we do less and/or different work?
- Reinvent who we are
  - Do we have the right skills for the future?
  - If not, how do we close the gap?
  - How do we engage everyone to do things without being told, to do more than expected, and to always follow up and follow through beyond the call of duty?
- Reinvent how we get our work done
  - How do we eliminate barriers between groups?
  - How do we engage individuals and groups to perform as teams, rather than as individual units with little collaboration?
  - How do we shift paradigms?
- Significantly improve communications
  - How do we clearly define and communicate priorities and accountabilities?
  - How can we communicate more effectively?
- Demonstrate greater leadership
  - How do we stay focused on the big picture and the issues relevant to meeting today's demands?
  - How do we create alignment and unleash potential?
  - How do we define roles, responsibilities, and boundaries as well as effective decision-making?

Chapter Eighteen | Alignment of the Organization and Its Employees

Alignment is the fit between individual needs and organizational requirements. The key to success for an organization will be to continue to create this fit between the individual and the company. But in many organizations over the preceding decade, commitment and the loyalty that accompanies it have been eroded or even destroyed by changes in structure and strategy.

The traditional employment contract and its tacit agreements have been broken. No longer do we have the "womb to tomb" career mentality, wherein an individual starts and ends his or her career in the same organization. People are more mobile and looking for different things at different stages of their careers. Productivity increases will depend upon the release of individual energies that will be possible only if real alignment is established throughout the organization.

Over the last 10 years we have developed an Organizational Effectiveness Model, which is used to develop alignment throughout organizations. It is also the backbone of how we implement assessment interviewing in organizations today.

There are six steps to the model of creating alignment and fit within an organization:

1. **Purpose:** Why we exist
2. **Values:** Who we are
3. **Business Road Map:** How we get there
4. **Alignment Road Map:** Agreed-upon purpose, values and business road map
5. **Personal Responsibility:** Unleashing the involvement and potential of each person
6. **Results:** Sustainable, quality performance

How can you learn how to "fit" or retain a person if the organization or the individuals in the organization are not clear on their purpose or values? How do you develop the fit between an individual and an organization if the organization and the individual are not clear on their direction? Working through each of these steps is critical in creating alignment and fit.

PURPOSE

At the organizational level, purpose is used to define why the organization exists and what business it is in. It is used to inspire people to want to be a part of something special that, therefore, can attract and retain better people. It provides clarity, focus, and direction.

Ironically, companies do spend time in developing these purpose or mission statements, yet they often spend no time aligning them throughout the organization. Just go to most any company and their recruiting department and ask people there about the purpose for their company. Many will go to their pockets and try to find the cards that have the statements written on them. Since the statements are not internalized and have little meaning for most of the people, how can they be used successfully by recruiters? Yet, for those people who have internalized these mission statements, they provide an enthusiasm that is contagious.

Companies that have been successful for long periods have mission statements that transcend time. They are as good today as when they were first defined. They withstand the test of time. Here are some examples:

- **Merck:** "We are in the business of preserving and improving human life. All of our actions must be measured by our success in achieving this goal."
- **Nordstrom:** "Service to the customer above all else."
- **Wal-Mart:** "We exist to provide value to our customers, to make their lives better via lower prices and greater selection; all else is secondary."
- **Fannie Mae:** "To strengthen the social fabric by continually democratizing home ownership."

Each of these statements of purpose or mission has withstood the test of time and still exists today. It is a beacon, a light that creates the journey to the future.

VALUES

Every decision made in an organization is based on a value. When there is conflict among people, it is usually based on a value. To develop trust, people must understand each other's values. Yet values are seen as the "soft side" of business.

A company's values reflect the criteria it has used in deciding its mission, management philosophy, and strategy, and they focus the efforts of its human resources. Values determine how an organization deals with its environment, both internally and externally, and how it operates. By examining an organization's values, people start to better understand the roles they play, the goals and objectives they set, the decisions they make, and how to effectively interact with suppliers, customers, competitors, employees, government, and others.

Think about some organizations that are considered winners. Walt Disney focuses on making people happy, Nike focuses on competition, and 3M focuses on innovation. These values are demonstrated throughout the organizations and in everything they do, from 3M giving employees an opportunity each week to innovate, to Nike endorsing those athletes who represent the best of competition, such as Michael Jordan and Tiger Woods. Winning organizations have strong values.

Winning leaders, too, clearly articulate a set of values for themselves. Leaders continually reflect on the values to make sure that they are appropriate for achieving the desired results. These kinds of leaders embody the values with their own behavior and encourage others to apply the values in their own decisions and actions, and they also aggressively confront and deal with pockets of ignorance and resistance.

Just as organizations must identify, clarify, and test their values, so must individuals. To the extent that every decision we make is based on a value, it is critical to understand the values of those people we bring into our organization. Otherwise, the likelihood that they will succeed will be minimized. This is essential to the alignment process.

BUSINESS ROAD MAP

The third element of this model is creating a *business road map*. Organizations use this to identify how they are going to achieve their purpose. Included in the road map are critical success factors, core competencies, and key business processes.

The critical success factors help determine the strategy by helping persons understand the marketplace or customers that need to be served. Without this knowledge, organizations may go down a path that leads them nowhere. This focus helps to determine what is required to be successful.

Core competencies identify what you must be great at to compete. Since you cannot be all things to all people, you have to focus on those areas that will make a difference. For example, in the changing financial services area, Hoopis Financial Group, the most successful general agency in the Northwestern Mutual Financial Network, had identified three core competencies: listening, relationship selling, and product knowledge and integration. In continuing his quest for excellence, Harry Hoopis has spent time and energy to transform his organization to meet the needs of a changing industry. These core competencies will impact this change.

Key business processes represent those that are used to design how the organization will look. We talk about processes as compared to functions to give them a dynamic focus rather than the traditional activities they represent. For example, in the financial services industry we focus on risk management, wealth accumulation, and wealth preservation to identify those areas of organizational focus together with the people process, the financial process and the administration process. We design the organization around these processes so each individual can see where he or she contributes to the overall enterprise.

Critical Measures for Success

Managers identify critical measures to help calibrate how the organization is performing on an ongoing basis. Measures in this area include: customer measures; operational measures; financial measures; and people measures.

ALIGNMENT

Alignment is critical. In an organization this is where agreement on the purpose, values, and road map occurs. There are three stages of reaching alignment.

The first stage is *compliance*, in which people do things because they are required to do them. If the boss says, "Jump" they ask, "How high?" If the boss says, "Run," they ask, "How far?" The problem with compliance is that it does not generate excitement or buy-in. It is done in accordance with what is asked for. Little creativity or ideas will be borne out at this level. One way to determine whether people are at this stage is when you hear them say, "This is what I ought to do or should be doing." This indicates that the individual does not have ownership of what he or she is being asked to do.

The second stage of alignment is *enrollment*, where individuals are starting to see the value or importance of what is being asked and start to see an impact or influence they might have.

The third stage of alignment is *commitment*, where people feel an ownership of the process and recognize the impact they can have. Here you will hear people say, "This is what I want or need to be doing." It is in this phase where creativity, new ideas, and challenging the process can and will occur.

The importance of building toward alignment is that it is a developmental process that achieves true results. People feel a sense of ownership and involvement that creates the buy-in to achieve what needs to be done. There is a sense of accomplishment, of being part of something, and of feeling that you contributed to the result. However, this is not a process of entitlement on the company's part. What the company is entitled to is *compliance*, and what it must earn is *commitment*.

This is reflected in the finding that some 65 percent of people within companies today are compliant, some 25 percent are enrolled, and about 10 percent are aligned or committed. To test this, just ask people about the purpose, the values, and/or the business road map of their company. Most will not know, and some will look for a paper that describes it in some fashion. Without alignment it is hard to see where individuals fit into the organization and the impact and influence they can have.

Alignment Questions

We can actually test for alignment by asking a series of questions in an evaluation interview. In Philip Crosby's model of "Quality as Absolutes," he uses five basic questions to test for the degree of alignment. It is important to understand that we each start off with a set of expectations as we tackle issues of concern, whether known or to be identified. The key is to understand our expectations and then start to set requirements and understandings of what they mean to each other. At the end of the conversation it is important to assess the degree of true understanding that exists. These five questions test for that level of understanding:

1. To what extent is the new set of mutual expectations *meaningful?*
2. To what extent is the new set of expectations *achievable?*
3. To what extent is the new set of expectations *clearly stated?*
4. To what extent is the new set of expectations *measurable?*
5. To what extent is the new set of expectations *agreed upon?*

The same questions can be used by individuals to test for alignment to see if what they are pursuing relative to their goals and objectives matches that of the organization. In like fashion, the organization looks to identify these principles when assessing a candidate's expectations and needs. It is at this stage where the fit occurs. We use the

Platinum Rule as we work with people. This states, "To the extent that we can understand and meet your needs, our needs will be met."

As a philosophy, this allows us to focus on the needs of people, as opposed to whether people are good or bad. If someone is not a fit for the organization, we can identify how, as an organization, we are not meeting what the individual is looking for. So, the assessment process is really an "alignment process," that is aligning people's skills, competencies, and values to the organization's values and the job description or opportunity to be filled. This is the same process that we use as we give feedback to people and attempt to set development plans.

PERSONAL RESPONSIBILITY

To the extent that we have created the alignment or fit for individuals and the organization, individuals can unleash their potential in what they do. They can take risks, challenge the status quo, and move to new heights, because they feel a part of the organization and believe in what the desired results are. They do not have to be micro-managed, because they share the same vision. They are clear on what needs to be done, and when it needs to be done, and feel enabled to do it. There is almost nothing to stop them from contributing because they are part of something special and, most important, they feel their contribution will make a difference. This can be observed by others in the excitement and the passion they bring to their work. In fact, it is not just work, but their life's work.

RESULTS

Results can be seen in sustainable measurements and quality performance. One of the keys here is sustainability. Organizations, like individuals, can have a good year or two, but the best organizations, like the best people, are able to sustain their performance over time.

The Organizational Effectiveness Model, while developed to be used within organizations, is the same model we use as we work with individuals. In this case we call it the Personal Effectiveness Model. If you were to go through each of the steps, you would find the direct corollary on an individual level. For people to be successful, they need to have a clear sense of their purpose, their calling, and what excites them each and every day. While most people are not crystal clear on this, they certainly have some ideas about what makes them happy and where they derive their pleasure.

As part of the assessment process, it is important to identify these themes and patterns. For some people there is a pattern of helping people, whether it was early work experiences in teaching tennis, being a teaching assistant, being a camp counselor, or helping to solve technical problems. To others, it might be a competitive edge from early involvement in sports or roles in sales. There is, in each person, that sense of purpose that is an integral part of who they are. Successful people, at any level, can share this "calling" with you.

RELATED RENEWALS

The key to organizational renewal and sustainability is the renewal of individual commitment to the organization and its future. Conceptually, organizational renewal focuses on the *reframing, recommitting,* and *renewing* of employees to the company and its objectives.

Reframing for employees means they must see themselves differently than before. They must assess their strengths and weaknesses and self-determine a career path and the "fit" of their abilities to the objectives and purpose of the company.

Recommitting is the second concept, which brings into focus the fit of the employees to the company, a rededication and re-energizing of their work commitment, and an acceptance of their roles.

Renewal is the product of reframing plus recommitment. The individual's spirit and enthusiasm are renewed and he or she, along with the company, is reinvigorated to maximum performance and goal attainment. Renewal of the organization occurs as the objectives of the company meld with employee recommitment. The intent is to move employees from "benefit consciousness" to "commitment consciousness." At the same time, the concept creates in the individual a responsibility for his or her career direction and development of the skills to achieve career goals.

Organizational renewal is really an evaluation process for the company and its employees to determine the fit (i.e., match of skills, interests, goals, etc.) of the employee to the company and its future. Through a process of evaluation, feedback, and career conferencing, mutual decisions are made for the best interests of both the employee and the company. Ultimately, renewal occurs because employees are rededicated to the company and they match more closely to their jobs and to the career paths available. The company prospers because employees are satisfied, productivity increases, and objectives are attained.

Although organizational renewal appears to fit best during times of change (expansion, restructuring, mergers, acquisitions, etc.), it is an excellent vehicle for maintaining company growth when upheaval is not occurring as well. In all instances, it is a proactive approach to human resource management and makes a significant positive impact on the organization. After full implementation has been completed, the renewal process becomes an integral part of human resource development and management. It will essentially eliminate the trauma that otherwise may be associated with any changes.

Management will have a better understanding of the strengths and weaknesses of employees and consequently be in an advantageous position to make decisions objectively and fairly for employees and the company. Further, employees will know where they fit and the long-term match of their skills and career aspirations to the company's objectives. Mutual agreement will be much more readily attained, and the typical negatives associated with employee movement will be significantly reduced.

THE UNIT OF RENEWAL

Current efforts to improve organizational effectiveness frequently begin with analysis of structures and functions, as they relate to specific job requirements. Judgments are made about the value of particular job functions in relation to overall organizational objectives from the individual who carries out the job. Such analysis may create a more efficient or rational organizational structure, but it cannot renew the energies necessary to improve the organization's sustained performance.

Only individual renewal of loyalty and commitment can create breakthroughs in productivity of the kind organizations now require. By focusing on the individual as the unit of renewal, the process outlined here ensures the organization's sustained results. But, it should be noted that such a process runs counter to the prevailing and currently popular ways of improving organizational performance.

By making the individual the center of the renewal process, we seek to counter this serious neglect. The countercultural nature of this renewal process around alignment is being stressed here for a reason. It is vital for the overall success of the renewal effort to have the commitment of top leadership to the process itself. When a process is, by nature, countercultural, leadership must be ready for chaos and turmoil. The beginning of any truly creative process is always messy, and wise leaders understand this to the point of encouraging the necessary disorder. Organizational renewal and transformation to achieve sustained results is not for the fainthearted.

LINKING ACTION

Actual placement of individuals into specific job functions is the work of this final phase and ensures the continuous fit. A culture of development is established, which stresses the fact that renewal and fit must be an ongoing process. No strategy, structure, or system can be allowed to develop as permanent. By emphasizing the temporary nature of these elements of organization, the primacy of the individual and his or her commitment can be asserted.

It is important to note that leadership is very much a quality of the commitment made by an individual and an organization, along with the demonstrated competencies that are required to fulfill the nature of the work. Aligning individual motivations, energies, and skills around an organization's purpose and values is the definition of leadership.

SUSTAINABLE PERFORMANCE

To the extent we are willing to follow a model that is as good for the organization as it is for the individual, we will have enhanced our ability to achieve alignment in an open and sincere manner. The Organizational Effectiveness Model demonstrated in this chapter works to achieve this goal. The alignment or fit factor is the key to sustainable performance, not only organizationally, but personally too.

Appendix A | The Evaluation Interview Guide

A STEP-BY-STEP LIST OF KEY INTERVIEW QUESTIONS

Introduction

"In our company we believe that the more we can learn about you the better we will be able to help you with your long-range career direction. So today, I would like to have you tell me everything you can about *your work experience, your education, and your outside interests.*"

Part 1. Work Experience

"Suppose you begin by telling me about your previous jobs, starting with the first job working up to the present. I would be interested in *how you got each job, what you did, your likes, your dislikes, earnings, and any achievements and disappointments along the way.* Where should we begin? How about some jobs you may have had in high school and college?"

A. The following questions (1-7) are asked for every job.
1. How did you get this job?
2. Duties and responsibilities?
3. Likes? Why?
4. Things found less satisfying? Why?
5. Level of earnings? (Note progress or lack thereof.)
6. What new skills did you acquire on this job?
7. Reasons for changing jobs?

B. The following questions (8-11) are asked after the most recent job is discussed.
8. What did you learn regarding your strengths as a result of working on those jobs? For example, did you find that you worked harder than the average person, got along better with people, organized things better? Tell me about your strengths.
9. On the other side, we each have areas where we can improve. What clues did you get as to your development needs as a result of working on these jobs?
10. What adjectives would peers (or boss/subordinates as applicable) use to describe you?
11. What does a job have to have to give you satisfaction? Some people look for money, some for security, some want a challenge. What is important to you?

C. Questions 12-20 are customized optional questions.
12. To what extent have you had the opportunity to demonstrate leadership? Give me an example.
13. Give me an example of a project you worked on, the issues that were identified, and the role you played.
14. What processes do you use that help make you effective as an engineer?
15. What is your definition of a team? Tell me about any opportunities you have had to work as a team member. Discuss the team's goals, accomplishments, and how conflicts were resolved.

16. Tell me about your current areas of expertise and how you have acted as a resource or advisor to others.
17. What single accomplishment are you most proud of and why?
18. On the other hand, each of us has had some disappointments. Identify one technical disappointment that stands out for you.
19. Where would you like to be in the next 1-3 years and 3-5 years?
20. What has prompted your interest in our industry and, specifically, our company?

D. For a person who has had varied experiences or when you are not sure what type of job the person is looking for, ask these questions.

21. In our company we have many different opportunities. (List examples.) Which would you prefer if you had your choice and why?
22. Give me three words that would best describe you.

At this point, ask your tandem interviewer, if any, what questions he or she has regarding work experience.

Part 2. Education and Training

"That gives me a good picture of your work experience. Now tell me something about your education. I would be interested in the *courses you like most, those you find less satisfying, the level of your grades, and your extra-curricular activities*. Start with high school and go on to college.

1. What courses did you enjoy most and why?
2. What courses did you find less satisfying and why?
3. What about grades? Were they average, above average, perhaps a little below average? What was your class rank?
4. How conscientious were you? Did you work about as hard as the average person, a little harder, or perhaps not quite so hard?
5. What were your SAT/ACT scores? GPA? GRE?
6. What colleges did you apply to? Which ones accepted you? Which one did you choose?

Repeat #1-4 for college

7. What training did you have beyond the undergraduate level?
8. To what extent have you had any continuing education past college?

At this point, ask your tandem interviewer what questions he or she has regarding education and training.

Part 3. Outside Activities and Interests

"Well, now, what are some of the things you like to do for fun and recreation, your hobbies and interests?"

1. Interests and hobbies
2. Sports
3. Reading
4. Community involvement

Wrap Up

"Well, that gives me an excellent picture of your background. I have enjoyed talking with you and want to thank you for coming. What one or two questions do you have for me?"

Appendix B | Evaluation Interview Note-Taking and Rating Forms

This appendix includes four forms, beginning on page 224, that facilitate taking notes during interviews and objectively rating candidates.

Appendix B.
Form 1. Work Experience (Downloadable Form)

Interviewee: _____

Interviewed by: _____   Date: _____

Clues	Job Title	Dates	Key Tasks/Responsibilities	Likes	Dislikes	Skills Acquired	Reasons for Leaving

Appendix B.
Form 2. Evaluation of Work Experience (Downloadable Form)

Strengths:	Weaknesses:
Adjectives:	
Job Satisfiers:	
Leadership:	
Safety:	
Quality:	
Teamwork:	
Supervisory Ability:	
Job Preferences:	
Structured/Unstructured	Why?
Theoretical/Practical	Why?
Detailed/Big Picture	Why?
Pressure/Not So Much	Why?
Key Accomplishments:	Key Disappointments:

Appendix B.
Form 3. Education/Well-Roundedness (Downloadable Form)

Grades/GPA	Likes	Dislikes	SAT/Standardized Test Scores	Schools Accepted by
High Schools: GPA: Colleges: GPA: Area of Study: Graduate School: GPA: Area of Study:				
Education Notes: Hobbies/Interests/Volunteering:				

Appendix B.
Form 4. Interview Rating Form (Downloadable Form)

(Best completed immediately after an interview)

Interviewee's Name: _____ Date: _____

Interviewer: _____ Tandem Note Taker: _____

Scoring 1-2-3-4-5 (1 being the lowest and 5 being the highest)

Gate 1

❏ Honesty (+ or -)

Gate 2

❏ Mental Ability   ❏ Motivation   ❏ Maturity

Gate 3

❏ Respect for Others	❏ Leadership	❏ Verbal Skills
❏ Hard Worker	❏ Initiative	❏ Team Worker
❏ Self-Discipline	❏ Listening	❏ Adaptability
❏ Self-Confidence	❏ Innovative	❏ Work Experience
❏ Impact	❏ Results-Oriented	❏ Analytical

❏ Builds Relationships

Summary of Assets

Summary of Shortcomings

Overall Summary/Additional Notes

| # Sample Report of Interview Findings

I. Work History

Samuel showed a strong work ethic and concern for people early in his career. During summers in high school, Samuel mowed lawns for a number of his neighbors. Although several were paying customers, Samuel did work free of charge for those who did not have the resources to personally care for their lawns.

While in college, Samuel was selected by a chemistry professor for an assistant's position. This reflects his high level of academic achievement, ability to develop relationships, and willingness to work hard. Samuel was compensated for 1/2 of his tuition costs, which amounted to approximately $700. In his senior year, he served as an academic advisor/counselor to undergraduate math and science majors. He demonstrated high energy and perseverance by working 30 hours per week, sometimes up to 40 hours, while maintaining a full course load. This position gave Samuel an opportunity to share his knowledge and expertise in math and science (4.0 GPA) while developing people-related skills of coaching and guiding others. He was compensated from 2/3 to 3/4 of his tuition costs. In this assignment, Samuel found working with other less academically accomplished in non-quantitative areas a challenge and sometimes frustrating.

Samuel applied and was accepted to a number of graduate schools, including Columbia University. However, he wanted to study under a specific professor at Princeton. Samuel demonstrated initiative and creativity when he wrote to the professor requesting his support for admission. The professor challenged Samuel to solve four problems as a prerequisite to a letter of recommendation. Samuel showed tenacity for goal accomplishment and risk-taking when he rejected admission to Columbia prior to receiving acceptance to Princeton. This was also against the advice of his parents.

Samuel followed this professor to New York University and was accepted with a full scholarship and a teaching assistantship in computer science. Samuel pursued this assistantship even though it was outside his areas of expertise in mathematics. His greatest challenge, proving stressful at times, was assimilating into a diverse culture and a different educational system. Samuel continued to excel academically and persevered in a highly competitive environment. In 1975, Samuel completed a Ph.D. in mathematics with a GPA of 4.0.

After completing his degree in 1975, Samuel followed the advice of another professor by applying for a faculty position at the University of Missouri. He was selected to teach math and computer science courses. After three years, Samuel was bored with the repetition of teaching and took the initiative to use summers and out-of-class time to pursue industry-related grants. Samuel's initiative and motivation to learn business applications proved fruitful. After several years of collaborating on projects, Samuel was pursued by McDonnell Douglas to work in the structural analysis function of engineering. Samuel excelled at utilizing his background in math and computer science to solve business problems. He received a series of promotions in this assignment, progressing from a Programmer Analyst to a Sr. Consultant in less than four years, a testament to his technical skills and ability to adapt to new situations. In 1986, Samuel's quick mental ability and strong interpersonal skills made him a candidate for promotion to Sr. Section Manager in Business Applications.

Learning to manage individuals with diverse backgrounds and skill sets was accomplished but with some disappointment. Peers, subordinates, and superiors recognize Samuel's intellect and ability to get things done but also feel that Samuel is impatient and demanding in relationships. Through this assignment Samuel honed his negotiation skills and customer orientation and was promoted to Manager of Business Appli-cations in record time (less than six months). His salary of $49K and consistently high merit increases reflected dramatic profit-oriented achievements and were commensurate with his management responsibilities of more than 85 employees.

In 1990, the Information Systems group was sold. Samuel had two external offers of employment. Instead of taking this risk, Samuel was persuaded by management to consider a position in MCAIR Information Technology. Samuel was selected as Branch Manager through a very competitive posting process. This was a lateral move, and there was no change in salary.

His new position differed significantly from former assignments. The focus was on managing people and processes. Due to downsizing and differences in organizational culture, Samuel had difficulty adapting to the MCAIR environment. Samuel clearly enjoyed the exposure to new technology and meeting new people. However, making difficult people-related decisions in absence of quantitative data was a challenge. Despite these barriers, Samuel was selected during the consolidation of MCAIR and MDMSC, to be one of four Directors in MDA Information Systems organization of Business Management. His salary in 1993 was $78K and he was approved for the incentive compensation program. His duties were to integrate systems, develop frameworks for applications, and establish IS standards for MDA. Software development life cycles, audits, security, and systems architecture were also key responsibilities. Samuel excelled in setting enterprise direction for technology but had difficulty balancing diverse customer needs and internal "politics." His knowledge of HR processes and the complexity of managing in a matrix structure was expanded as a function of this job.

Although extremely effective at managing costs and profit/loss, Samuel lacked strong leadership skills. Coaching and counseling subordinates to achieve outstanding results were not as easily mastered as technical skills. He was not as skilled as desirable in developing strong peer relationships and influencing others. Results from the Profilor management assessment tool seem to substantiate this as an area in need of development.

During his tenure in this assignment, Samuel was selected from a diverse group of high performers to complete for the Division Leadership Development Track IV (DLDT) Program. This enhanced his peer relationships and gave him a broader perspective of the enterprise. Samuel left this assignment when leadership changed in the Business Management organization and he had an opportunity in the Process Audit organization. He was identified for this assignment by the Vice President of Process Audit from a pool of high-performing employees. This position has given Samuel the opportunity to develop a new skill set in manufacturing and obtain experience in other MDC locations. Samuel is utilizing problem solving, relationship building, and assertiveness in this assignment. Samuel is currently evaluating his career goals and anticipates having a formal career plan developed in the next 30 days.

II. Education and Training

Samuel has a superior academic record. He consistently attained a 4.0 GPA at the undergraduate and graduate level through completion of his Ph.D. As mentioned previously, Samuel was accepted by multiple institutions with high academic standards. His standing in high school through graduate school is reported to be nothing less than "first in class" all the while working 20-30 hours per week. This is strong evidence of his outstanding mental ability and high energy.

Samuel has diverse academic interests. Obviously he excels in analytical subjects such as math and physics but also enjoys and achieves in literature, drama, and poetry. History, anthropology, and more courses of study such as art were not of interest but clearly did not impact his academic achievements. Samuel clearly excels in academic settings.

III. Present Social Adjustment

While busy working and going to school, Samuel has maintained a marriage and has children. Samuel enjoys activities such as tennis, listening to classical music, and watching sports on TV. He also enjoys non-traditional activities such as cooking and researching medical technologies. These activities display Samuel's value for competition and autonomy.

IV. Summary of Strengths and Areas to Improve

Summary of Assets	Summary of Shortcomings
Superior mental ability	**Develop leadership skills**
learns quickly	assertiveness and self-direction
articulate	translate vision into action
intellectual depth and diversity	mental toughness
problem solver	
Outstanding motivation	**People skills**
high energy	tolerance for diversity of ability
hard worker	manage through relationships
sets high standards	patience
Maturity	**Self-promotion**
good judgment	tolerance for diversity of ability
hard worker	manage through relationships
sets high standards	
People skills	**Conflict resolution**
tactful	avoids confrontation even when right
sensitive	
friendly	
Character	
honest	
adaptable	
Customer focus	
entrepreneurial	
results oriented	

V. Summary

Samuel's intellectual ability and energy surpass most of his contemporaries. He has a very strong work ethic, adapts quickly to new environments, is articulate, and has diverse interests as well as achievements. A focus and tenacity for achieving results produces high levels of satisfaction and commitment from Samuel's customers.

Throughout his career Samuel has expressed a desire to work with others. He has the ability to form warm, meaningful interpersonal relationships. However, his mental agility and occasional impatience with those less gifted in math and science are a handicap to managing subordinates. Samuel sets high standards for himself and is frustrated when others do not live up to these standards. Further, bureaucratic cultures driven by relationships do not energize Samuel or permit him the level of control he desires. Samuel has an entrepreneurial spirit that thrives on variety, innovation, and high energy. A small to mid-size technical operation (division or subdivision) focused on the external customer/supplier is the best match for Samuel's capacity for high mental stimulation and people interaction.

Appendix D

Guidelines for Giving and Receiving Feedback

FEEDBACK

Feedback is a continuous process of active communication offering and asking for help with an expectation to achieve an agreed-upon desired outcome.

Model for Receiving Enabling Feedback

Awareness through listening.

Assess through understanding.

Action on agreement.

Guidelines for Receiving Enabling Feedback

- Be open and receptive.
- Be objective, not defensive.
- Actively listen to what is said and why.
- Ask for clarification for understanding.

Appendix D. Guidelines for Feedback

- Agree upon what actions need to be taken by whom and by when.
- Collaborate on solutions.
- Recognize continuous improvement opportunities.

Model for Giving Feedback

Describe the behavior.

Express how you feel about it.

Specify what you want to reinforce, build on, or to change and collaborate with the receiver to create learning opportunities.

Summarize in a positive way and seek out responses for understanding and agreed-upon actions to be taken.

Guidelines for Giving Feedback

- Set goals, expectations, and outcomes (consequences).
  - Be specific.
  - Be objective.
  - Be realistic.
  - Be measurable.
  - Be value-anchored.
  - Be immediate/timely.
- Consider the place and surroundings.
- Plan what you want to say (approach).
- Listen to and observe the person receiving your feedback.
- Give the receiver a chance to respond.

Index